# Stoicism

*Stoic Wisdom to Gain Confidence, Calmness and Control Your Emotions. Stop Anxiety and Depression in Modern World. Develop Unbelievable Self Discipline and Discover Stoicism Philosophy.*

© **Copyright 2019 by Tony Bennis - All rights reserved.**

The content contained within this book may not be reproduced, duplicated or transmitted without direct written permission from the author or the publisher.

Under no circumstances will any blame or legal responsibility be held against the publisher, or author, for any damages, reparation, or monetary loss due to the information contained within this book, either directly or indirectly.

Legal Notice:

This book is copyright protected. It is only for personal use. You cannot amend, distribute, sell, use, quote or paraphrase any part, or the content within this book, without the consent of the author or publisher.

Disclaimer Notice:

Please note the information contained within this document is for educational and entertainment purposes only. All effort has been executed to present accurate, up to date, reliable, complete information. No warranties of any kind are declared or implied. Readers acknowledge that the author is not engaging in the rendering of legal, financial, medical or professional advice. The content within this book has been derived from various sources. Please consult a licensed professional before attempting any techniques outlined in this book.

By reading this document, the reader agrees that under no circumstances is the author responsible for any losses, direct or indirect, that are incurred as a result of the use of information contained within this document, including, but not limited to, errors, omissions, or inaccuracies.

# Table of Contents

*Introduction: Taking Control in a World That Seems Out of Control...........5*

*Chapter 1: Stoicism 101...............................9*

*Chapter 2: History of Stoicism..................23*

*Chapter 3: The Power of Perception..........35*

*Chapter 4: Healthy and Unhealthy Passions.................................................47*

*Chapter 5: Taking Action...........................61*

*Chapter 6: Viewing the World Through a Stoic Lens.................................................76*

*Chapter 7: Living in Accordance with Nature....................................................89*

*Chapter 8: Stoicism and Psychology........101*

*Chapter 9: Accepting the Unacceptable..............................................114*

*Chapter 10: Stoicism in Practice..............125*

*Conclusion: A Philosophy for Life............137*

*References..................................................140*

# Introduction: Taking Control in a World That Seems Out of Control

We should be in control.

We are living in an era where humans have learned to harness and command the forces of nature in ways that would make us look divine to ancient men. We can fly through the sky like Apollo, we can send messages faster than Hermes could ever have dreamed, and our nuclear power plants can put Zeus and his lightning bolts to shame.

So, why is it that the average person feels like they are losing control rather than gaining it?

Humanity has been able to transform so many things since the ancient Greeks, but one of the few things that hasn't changed is human nature itself. Technology has grown by leaps and bounds while human evolution continues to move at a snail's pace.

We as a species have been so caught up trying to control the external world that many of us never find the time to look inward. It's so easy to think that if we make a little more money, convince more people to like us, or lose some stomach fat then we'll finally achieve happiness and control.

Take a moment to think of all the great and powerful men and women who seemed to have it all, but ended up losing everything because of poor decisions or emotional issues?

You probably don't need to think for long to come up with an impressive list. History is filled with such tragic tales. But what's even worse is all the untold stories of personal tragedies suffered by individuals who didn't make the history books. We all have our personal demons, but far too many people fall victim to them without ever facing them.

If you want to achieve real confidence, serenity, and control in your life then you need to stop trying to control the world around you and start getting control of yourself.

That is what stoicism is all about. It might be an ancient philosophy, but the needs it addresses are still as real as they ever were. A Roman soldier with a gladius in his hands might look completely different from a modern soldier with a rifle in their hands, but the thoughts and emotions going through their minds would be similar.

It's easy to think that because the world of today is changing so quickly, we must need ideas that are as trendy as our gadgets. But so far, no technology has been invented that fundamentally changed human nature or the human mind. You may have a smartphone, a car, and a robot that vacuums your house, but your brain would look just like the brain of an ancient Roman Emperor.

That's why so many modern people are looking back to the wisdom of the ancients. They want to find out the solutions to these eternal problems that were devised by people who weren't distracted by modern technology. The ancient stoics couldn't count on an app to solve their problems, they couldn't look for a chemical to reprogram their brain, and they definitely couldn't hope to achieve eternal life using cryogenic stasis. They had to use their innate human skills and capacities to take control of themselves.

This doesn't mean that modern stoics have to be luddites who forsake all technology. Modern science and medicine are wonderful things. Don't think for a second that any philosophy can replace a trip to the doctor. But any scientist or doctor will tell you that there are also limits to their trades. Science can explain how life works and doctors can help you live a healthy life, but neither science nor medicine can explain the meaning of life. That is a philosophical question.

While science has helped us to achieve many wonderful things, it still has its limitations. The truth is that even with all of the advances in modern technology we're still worlds away from achieving anything close to complete control of the world around us. And even if we could control matter and energy, it wouldn't change our basic emotions and thought patterns.

So many things in this life will never be in your control. The one thing you can truly command in this world is yourself. In this book we will show you how to take control of your mind, and once you have that control you can begin to take control of your life.

Stoicism can't promise you a perfect life. It can't promise you a healthy life. But if you take the time to study it carefully and put its concepts into practice then you can meet the ups and downs of life with wisdom and perspective. Rather than being tossed through life like a log in a rushing river, you can take command and chart your own route forward.

The power to change is within you. The path to enlightenment has been written out for you for thousands of years. It's just a matter of taking in that ancient wisdom and putting it into practice. If you can take those steps, then you can see your life transform from the inside out.

# Chapter 1: Stoicism 101

*Man conquers the world by conquering himself.*

—Zeno of Citium

Before we dive into the specifics of Stoicism it will be helpful to take a look at the big picture. Think of it as looking at a map of a city before you decide to start driving down the individual streets.

In this chapter, we will look at what Stoicism is and isn't in the broadest terms. Once we are finished with this step, you'll be ready to dive into the more specific details of this philosophical system and the practical ways you can put it to use in your life.

Let's begin your Stoic journey.

## A Way of Life

Stoicism is a philosophy. This might sound painfully obvious, but the truth is that most modern people have a very loose understanding of what a philosophy is. Most people would say that it's a system for thinking about the world around them, when the reality is that it is so much more.

Philosophers have always been defined by the way they think about the world. They're obsessed with carefully and systematically considering their beliefs. But this process isn't just thinking for the sake of thinking. Socrates, the father of Western philosophy, made it clear that the ultimate goal of philosophy was to live a good life. The idea was that you thought through questions of ethics, logic, and meaning in careful ways so that you could live the best life possible.

The ancient Stoics believed that it wasn't enough to simply hold the right beliefs, you needed to put those beliefs into practice.

So, with that in mind, we can examine exactly what Stoics believe by exploring the different ways they approach life.

**Living in Accordance with Reality**

Stoicism is a philosophy that is filled with ideas that seem simple enough but can be quite complex in practice. This begins with the idea that a Stoic should accept reality as it is.

Few people believe that they are living in rebellion against reality. We walk around with our eyes and ears open and take in what is around us. What could be simpler than that?

But the Stoic emphasizes the importance of beliefs. Most of us filter what we take in through a reality distorting lens of belief. We are quick to apply labels like "good" and "bad," "right" and "wrong." Human nature drives people to apply quick and clean labels to everything they come in contact with, but Stoicism points out that this can make it difficult to live with the world as it really is when we get so caught up on what it should be.

This doesn't mean that Stoics are moral relativists who believe that moral questions are meaningless. As we will see later, questions around virtue are key to Stoic philosophy. Rather, the Stoics believe that our drive to label things as soon as possible actually creates many problems and makes it difficult for us to meaningfully address other issues.

Ask yourself this question, how many times have you let a problem get out of control because you convinced yourself that it wasn't really a problem and just ignored it? Or how many times have you gotten yourself worked up over an issue that you labeled as insurmountable, only to find that it wasn't such a big deal after you actually got to work addressing it?

The average person suffers a life filled with self-inflicted wounds due to their inability to deal with reality as it is. Our emotions turn mountains into molehills and molehills into mountains. The Stoic solution is to examine the world through dispassionate eyes.

## Living in Acceptance of Fate

Another central point of Stoicism is the supremacy of fate. It's easy to see this as the belief that life is beyond your control, but it's actually about recognizing the limits of your control. The Stoics believed that every human only controls one thing in this giant and unbelievably complex world: their own mind.

Some people hear this and view it as depressing. Humans naturally overestimate what they're in control of. Consider the fact that so many sports fans think that the clothing they wear might be the ultimate deciding factor in how their favorite team performs in the big game. Being reminded of the fact that this is false might be seen as frustrating to a fan who feels helpless without such agency, but it can also allow them to claim agency in other areas.

So many people spend their entire lives trying to control things that they have no power over while ignoring the things that they can control. Think about all of the people locked in unhealthy relationships where they struggle to change their partner while they make no effort to change themselves or break things off and seek out someone who is more compatible.

You cannot control other people. There might be things you can do to influence them, but you can never have anything close to the same level of control that you have over yourself. Even still, if you try and take control over your own thoughts and actions, you'll likely realize you're not in complete command.

Stoicism is about letting go of what you can't control and focusing on what you can. This is what acceptance of fate means. The great irony is that only when you accept your limitations will you be able to achieve your full potential.

## Living in Pursuit of Virtue

One thing that often gets lost when people present more "self-help" oriented versions of Stoicism is the emphasis that the ancient Stoics placed on virtue. They believed that being a Stoic meant more than just standing firm and maintaining a stiff upper lip. Many would point out that this sort of behavior wasn't invented by their philosophers and could be seen in the behavior of all sorts of people. What separated a capital *S* Stoic from someone with lowercase *s* stoicism was this emphasis.

The word "virtue" is one of those terms that sounds simple enough until you try and carefully define what it means. Most people agree that we should be virtuous but there are big disagreements about what that means. For the sake of this introduction we will define virtue as living a life that exemplifies certain qualities.

## The Four Virtuous Qualities

1. Wisdom
2. Courage
3. Self-Control
4. Justice

A cursory reading of Stoic literature might lead you to believe that Stoicism is a negative philosophy, focusing on what you should avoid. But this couldn't be further from the truth. Stoicism isn't just about avoiding destructive passions, it's also about cultivating positive virtues. Any understanding that focuses on just one side of this equation is incomplete and misleading.

## Constant Development

The final thing you should understand about Stoicism is one of the most important, the Stoic's answer to the biggest question in the universe: what is the meaning of life?

Stoicism says that we are on this earth so that we can develop our virtues with every opportunity we are given. It says that every circumstance, no matter how positive or negative it might appear at first glance, offers us an opportunity to grow and improve as human beings. We do this by shedding negative passions, building personal virtues, and living in line with nature.

So, you see, every individual part of Stoicism comes together in the end to form a greater whole. Sure, it's about persevering through difficult times, but it is also about so much more. It's about living an active and productive life that produces happiness and good health. It's about making the best of life when circumstances seem bad and making the most of life when things seem to be going smoothly.

Stoicism is a way of seeing the world, a way of living life, and a way of making sure that once you reach the end you have no regrets to speak of.

## Defining the Terms

In this book you will run into a number of terms that are both highly important and used in very particular ways. Stoicism has a rich lexicon of terminology that you need to be able to understand if you want to make sense of the philosophy. While some Stoics use a heavy amount of Greek and Latin lingo, in this book we'll generally stick to the most common English translations so that the message is as easy to understand as possible.

### Passion

One thing you have to understand is that Stoicism often involves words that are used a certain way in normal life but take on a special meaning when used in the context of stoic philosophy. Passion is one of these words.

When used in normal life, passion usually has positive connotations, but in Stoicism passion is generally negative. Stoics use the word passion to refer to negative emotions. These are emotions that lead people away from virtue and towards vice. Passions are emotions that are to be shunned and downplayed as Stoics try to emphasize more virtuous emotions.

### Fate

The ancient Stoics believed in a more literal sense of fate as a grand plan for the universe that everyone had a part to play in. But in modern Stoicism, fate is generally understood to be everything that is beyond our control as individuals. You can control the actions that you take, but fate is in command of what those around you might choose to do. Acceptance of fate is an important part of Stoicism, with the idea being that it helps you focus on what you can control rather than all the things that are beyond your command.

## Virtue

This term was already mentioned in the last segment but it's worth going over again. Stoics taught that virtue is the point of life and the ultimate good. Virtue is a large idea that is made up of smaller ideas. These are the wisdom to know how to act, the courage to take proper action, the self-control necessary to restrain yourself from acting improperly, and the justice necessary to deal with others fairly and constructively. You can understand living virtuously as acting and thinking in the right manner.

Of course, what is good is a question beyond the scope of this book. Because this is a book that is designed to be used for people of all beliefs and walks of life, we will keep the use of this term somewhat vague. Hopefully you have your own moral and ethical beliefs that you can consider when the topic of virtue comes to mind. If you don't, then now would be a good time to do some soul searching to determine what you truly believe about right and wrong, good and evil.

## Sage

A sage is a Stoic who has achieved enlightenment. They have been able to throw off the shackles of passion and live in perfect harmony with nature. They have conquered illogic and come to possess perfect reason and happiness. This is the stage that every Stoic strived to reach, but almost none ever achieved.

There is a question of whether or not it's realistic to hope to actually achieve Sage status, but even if it isn't it's still worthwhile as an ideal that people can strive for as they practice Stoicism. The Stoic sage can thus be seen as a conceptual ideal of how people should be, set up so that we might all know what we should work towards (Pigliucci, 2017).

**What Stoicism Isn't**

They say a little wisdom can be more dangerous than ignorance. That goes for many things in life, and it's especially true with stoicism. The philosophy isn't too difficult to understand but many people still come to faulty conclusions based on their limited understanding. Sometimes understanding requires more than knowing what something is, you must also understand what it is not. That's why this section is here.

Let's dispel some of the most common myths surrounding stoicism.

## Stoicism isn't About Accepting Everything as it is

Too many people think that stoics are doormats that people can walk all over. The word can conjure an image of the guards at Buckingham Palace who are tasked with standing completely still. Even when tourists act like jerks and maniacs, the guard's job is to show no emotions. But anyone who has tried to actually touch one of those guards will tell you when a line is crossed, they act with force. The same goes for stoics.

Stoicism is about accepting things as they are, but that doesn't mean that you can't work to change things. Stoic acceptance is all about seeing the world as it truly is so that you can act correctly. If your house is on fire, the first thing you need to do is accept that your house is on fire. Pretending that everything is fine won't save your property, it will only keep you from taking the actions necessary to limit the damage.

The most famous stoic philosopher, Marcus Aurelius, was the emperor of the world's largest superpower. Modern proponents of the philosophy include artists, professional athletes, and CEOs. While you don't have to be incredibly ambitious to be a stoic, you shouldn't feel like stoicism might hold you back from achieving your goals. In reality it's the exact opposite, stoicism can help you change the world by helping you to change yourself.

## Stoicism isn't About Having No Emotions

It's easy to picture stoics as robots.

Stoicism isn't about eliminating emotions, it's about learning to control them. The stoic is like an emotional gardener, nourishing emotions that they want to see grow while working against unwanted emotions. Just as plants will always need water and weeds will always keep coming back, emotions never fully go away. But a stoic is like a person with a garden that has been carefully cultivated to serve their needs, while so many people have allowed their mental gardens to grow wild with all sorts of weeds.

So, if you're worried about becoming a robot, you can put your worries to rest. If you were hoping to become a robot, then I'm sorry to let you down. But if you learn and follow the path of stoicism you will learn that your emotions don't need to be your enemies. They can also be used to propel you to unknown heights.

## Stoicism isn't for Just One Type of Person

While the other misconceptions we have looked at before tending to come from people who haven't studied Stoicism, this is an idea that is all too often spread by people who study Stoicism. They like it so much that it becomes a part of their identity. This leads them to become overly protective, constantly on the lookout for anyone who might violate their cherished system of beliefs.

Some of these individuals are academics who are unhappy with the modern popularization of stoicism. They view it as a "watered down" form of Stoicism. They'll also say that it strays too far away from the original thinkers.

This view is trickier to refute because there is some truth to it. Popular Stoicism can be quite different from the Stoicism that was practiced by Zeno of Citium. But the fact is that different branches within stoicism began to pop up shortly after its founder died. Throughout the history of the school it's easy to recognize Stoicism as a practical philosophy rather than a dogma. While some fundamental truths should remain, it makes sense that people would adapt the beliefs to their time and purposes, just as the Romans did when they adopted Stoicism from the Greeks.

**Moving Forward**

One of the lessons of Stoicism is that we must put aside our preconceived notions if we are to see the world as it truly is. That also goes for studying Stoicism. Try to put aside whatever assumptions you might have based on passing references. If you come in with an open mind, then you are more likely to see the changes you're looking for when all is said and done.

**Practical Takeaway**

In this book you will be provided with plenty of information about what stoicism is, but did you pick up this book to learn about the history of philosophy?

Or do you want to change your life? If you want to see real change then you'll need to act.

For this reason, every chapter will end with practical advice that you can act on while you read the book. Most of them will only require some paper, a writing utensil, and a few minutes of your time. You can also write on a computer, but studies have shown that people are more likely to retain information that they have written by hand.

We'll start with something especially simple. Take your paper and writing utensil. Now, put the book down and write down all the most important points you learned from this chapter. Only the highlights, this shouldn't take more than a minute or two.

And go!

Alright, congratulations. You've just taken more action towards self-improvement than 90% of people who read these kinds of books. For extra credit you can skim through the chapter and compare it with your notes, looking for anything big you might have missed.

The world is filled with individuals who read countless books about self-improvement and never actually seem to achieve what they wanted. I would propose that this happens because people let information wash over them rather than internalizing it. And if they do take the time to internalize it, they never act on the information.

I propose there are three fundamental elements of growth:

1. Information
2. Internalization
3. Implementation

Books can provide you with information, but you have to handle the other two elements. What you get out of this book depends entirely upon what you're willing to do with the things you learn.

# Chapter 2: History of Stoicism

*A Stoic is someone who transforms fear into prudence, pain into transformation, mistakes into initiation, and desire into undertaking.*

—Taleb Nassim Nicholas

It's important to be clear that this book isn't a textbook about the history of stoicism and the many great thinkers that contributed to it. Many of these books already exist and if you desire an in-depth examination of the details of the history of Western philosophy then they are worth reading.

This book is about practical stoicism. The goal is providing you with the information you need to start improving your life as soon as possible. This means that we can't spend too long on historical details, but it doesn't mean that we can ignore them.

In this chapter, we will be taking a quick tour through the history of stoicism. We'll examine its creation in ancient Greece, it's culmination in Imperial Rome, and the modern revival that has brought this ancient philosophy back to the forefront of intellectual discourse.

A single chapter can't provide you with everything there is to learn, but it can be a good jumping-off-point from which you can go on to dig into this rich and fascinating topic.

# Ancient Origins

Stoicism was founded in the cradle of Western philosophy, ancient Greece. In the fourth century BC, there was a well-off trader by the name of Zeno of Citium. While he was trading, he became shipwrecked near the city state of Athens. This type of misfortune has broken many men, but Zeno found opportunity in his suffering. He traveled to Athens and began to study at the feet of the local philosophers. He was seeking something that would satisfy him in a way that his material wealth hadn't. Ultimately, he would find his own sense of meaning, and he shared what he had learned with those who would listen.

Stoicism was founded to strike a balance between the extremes of Athenian philosophy. The Aristotelians preached that material wealth was necessary for enlightenment, while the Cynics boasted in their self-imposed poverty. Zeno struck that balance by moving the focus away from the material things that people have and onto their beliefs, values, and actions. He would spread his philosophy while standing atop a raised area known as the Stoa Poikile. This area would become known as the first school of Stoicism and would also give the philosophy its name.

It's also important to understand Stoicism as a product of history. This highly practical philosophy emerged during a period of great turmoil, hardship, and uncertainty in Greece. While Stoicism was founded in the fourth century BC it rose to prominence during the third century, following the aftermath of Alexander the Great's death and the drama that this created in the area. Many Greeks had placed their hopes on Alexander, and his quick and glorious rise to power looked like it might bring peace and prosperity to the Mediterranean and the surrounding regions for years to come. Then Alexander died suddenly and at a young age, creating a power vacuum that would lead to division and strife.

With time, Greece's power in the Mediterranean waned, while a small city-state known as Rome saw its power wax. It's important to note that the Greeks and Romans were very different in many respects, but the Romans still drew plenty of inspiration from their Grecian predecessors. The Romans looked to the Greeks for inspiration in the realms of art, religion, and philosophy. This is how stoicism made the leap from Greece to Rome.

As you can see, ancient stoicism didn't appear out of thin air. It was developed over centuries by a chain of great thinkers. Still, there is one man whose name has become synonymous with this philosophical school. All of the names listed thus far are worth knowing, but next we will look at one name you absolutely must remember.

While we think of modern philosophers as academics who are far from the seat of power, in ancient Greece they became deeply involved with politics and government. This helped elevate their status and spread their message for a time, but politics is a fickle business. Between the years of 88 and 86 BC war broke out and Athens was defeated. Many philosophers left and fled to Rome, signaling a shift eastward for Western philosophy (Pigliucci, n.d.).

In Rome the stoic philosophy would further develop. Many of the fundamentals would remain, but a greater emphasis was put on how stoicism could be applied to dealing with real life problems. Stoics like Seneca and Marcus Aurelius weren't just thinkers or teachers, they were active in Roman trade and politics. They needed a philosophy that could help them with tough decisions and trying times.

### Marcus Aurelius

All of the groundwork put in place by the original stoics lead to what many would consider to be an unlikely conclusion. Stoicism was a philosophy developed so that people could weather the storms of misfortune, so few people would guess that the man who would understand it most keenly and put it into practice with the greatest precision would be a man who should have been beyond suffering.

In the Ancient world of the Roman Empire and its neighboring territories, there was probably no one more envied than the Emperor. Ever since the fall of the Roman Republic the Emperor had become a man with power and prestige that many modern rulers would envy. So, how is it that a man who enjoyed unparalleled power, wealth, and respect came to produce what many consider to be the textbook for weathering pain and strife?

The story of Marcus Aurelius, as well as the writing he produced, is a reminder that the way we see the world is often distorted. We look at the great marble statues left behind by the Romans and imagine that the people were just as grand and superhuman. But the truth is that every person suffers many of the same struggles. Wealth, power, and fame can certainly equip you to handle certain challenges better than you would be able to without these privileges, but they cannot completely erase struggle from your life.

**Marcus Aurelius's Biography**

The boy who would become emperor, Marcus Aurelius, did not have a particularly auspicious birth. He was born into a rich and powerful family, but there were many such families in Rome and Marcus' parents would never have predicted that he might become emperor. He only gained that title due to a series of improbable events.

Marcus was born under the rule of Emperor Hadrian. Since Hadrian had no biological heirs, he had to pick who would become Emperor after him. The first man he chose was Lucius Ceionius, but fate had it that Lucius would pass before the dying emperor. So, Hadrian had to pick again, and this time he chose a fellow childless man, a senator named Antonius Pius.

Pius sought to avoid the trouble that Hadrian had gone through, so he looked to adopt men who might be trained to succeed him. One of the boys he chose was Marcus and the other was named Lucius (Encyclopedia of World Biography).

It was as if the heavens had opened up and sent their blessings down upon young Marcus. Suddenly, his education was taken to a whole new level. He wasn't just in training to be a noble, he was training to be the most powerful man in Rome. To serve in this role, he studied under some of Rome's leading speakers and philosophers, all seeking to pour their wisdom into Marcus before the day he would take the throne. It was a high-stakes situation, nobody could know when the emperor might pass.

Marcus and his adopted brother took the throne as co-Emperors when Pius died in 161 BC. Their rule got off to a rocky start, as Rome was quickly plunged into the Parthian war. Rome would come out victorious, but at a disastrous cost. As the victorious legions returned to Rome, they carried the plague. Around five million Romans would be killed by the illness as Rome became a hothouse of deadly disease.

Shortly after the plague subsided Marcus's brother died, putting Marcus on the throne as the sole emperor of Rome. He would rule from 169 to 180. This 11 years was marked by war, social instability, and other troubles. But Marcus reigned with a steady hand and was later declared as the final member of the Five Good Emperors (Farnum Street).

So, you see that despite all of the power held by the Roman emperor, there was just as much responsibility. The fate of one of the world's greatest powers rested on Marcus' shoulders. Many of the men who took up this position cracked under pressure. Many swallowed their own propaganda and believed themselves to be above mere mortals. But Marcus was able to stand firm and lead Rome through the darkness with the help of his stoic virtues.

We know this because he recorded his thoughts. It gives us a rare chance to peer into the mind of one of history's great rulers.

**Meditations**

While Marcus Aurelius achieved many things during his time as Emperor, in the end it is his writing that has been his longest lasting achievement. When Marcus was out on the battlefield leading his soldiers in defense of Rome, he began to write notes. The amazing thing about the book is that he didn't write it to be published. It was a journal to him, but after his death it was recognized as one of the greatest works of stoic philosophy ever created.

The book is a series of quotes that were written down by Marcus as a reminder to himself. The Emperor himself never gave the book a title, so you need to understand the Meditations is a descriptive title that has been given to the work by those who discovered his writings later on.

*Meditations* is divided into twelve different sections, but these parts aren't ordered chronologically or thematically. This makes reading *Meditations* a unique experience. It's more like a book of quotations or the Biblical book of Psalms rather than a traditional narrative or textbook. This could be seen as one of the reasons for Meditations' popularity, it's a book that always has some wisdom to offer no matter what page you open up.

While the book isn't structured like most books are, some interesting patterns do arise. For one thing, at the start of the book he begins by thanking the people who have helped him throughout his life and shaped him as a thinker. This is a remarkable reminder of the fact that even the most powerful people on earth wouldn't be able to enjoy their positions without the wisdom and guidance of others. What we see in *Meditations* is the inner monologue of a true lifelong learner.

Another theme that quickly arises is the limitations of power and wealth. It's clear that while Marcus enjoyed more power than just about anyone else in the empire, he also felt his responsibility as a great weight. Reading *Meditations* is a humbling reminder of the struggles any good leader must deal with as they try and make the best of every situation.

If you finish this book and decide that you are interested in learning more about Stoicism from primary sources, then you should definitely consider picking up *Meditations* by Marcus Aurelius. If you get a modern translation, you'll find that this book is easy to read but difficult to fully grasp. You could spend decades studying this book and still find new insights with each readthrough.

## Modern Stoicism

Marcus Aurelius's *Meditations* is often considered to be the last great work of ancient stoicism. After his reign, the rigid school of thought faded away. However, this doesn't mean that stoic thought disappeared. On the contrary, stoic beliefs spread and were passed down. When the Empire converted to Christianity many Christian thinkers were drawn to works like *Meditations* and drew from its pages. Generations and generations of great thinkers were influenced by stoicism, even if they didn't know the name of the philosophy that had produced some of their most cherished ideas.

One of the things that modern stoics have done is dig through the ancient philosophy to try and find the insights that are most applicable to modern audiences. The ancient stoics were some of the most highly educated individuals in the Roman world, but they were still operating with the limited knowledge of the time. They could access their emotions just as we could, but they couldn't know the link between electrical currents in our brains and the way we feel.

Modern stoics have been able to use the tools of science and technology to gain greater insight into the fundamental breakthroughs made by those ancient thinkers. The past and the present collide in new and fascinating ways with each new wave of stoic thought.

One of the reasons why Stoicism feels as alive and powerful today as it did all those centuries ago is the fact that our modern circumstances mirror the situation in ancient Rome and Greece in some ways. Just as Stoicism originally came to be popular during a time of great uncertainty in Greece, it has enjoyed its modern revival as the world experiences its own struggles. In many ways we are living in an era that is more prosperous than ever, but we are also living in a time when people are dealing with many practical and existential struggles.

Despite the wealth that many nations show on paper, people still struggle with things like personal debt, healthcare costs, political divisions, questions surrounding climate change, and a struggle for personal meaning. Many people simply do not feel that modern life is all that they have been promised and even those who do enjoy wealth feel as though it is meaningless or transitory.

The economic engines of the Western world may have brought us many wonderful things, but it is clear that they have not fulfilled us in the way that many thought they would. It turns out that humans have deep needs that can't always be fulfilled by more money and the latest gadgets. The more things change, the more we find ourselves dealing with the same problems that the ancient Greeks were able to diagnose thousands of years ago. Once we recognize their perceptive abilities, it only makes sense that we might consider the solutions they offered.

While many surface-level changes have taken place, human nature remains much the same as it was two thousand years ago. The ancient stoics may be dead, but their ideas are as alive and vital as ever. Too many people get caught up in the language barrier that tends to get between modern readers and ancient texts. That's why books like this exist. The fundamental truths in this book aren't new, but they are being written so a modern audience can understand them clearly and apply them to solving contemporary issues. This book isn't about reinventing the wheel, it's about pushing a wheel forward that has been turning for thousands of years.

Philosophy isn't about worshipping the thoughts of ancient philosophers and treating their ideas as untouchable. It's about the living legacy of these ideas. We return to the wisdom of the ancients because they are the ones who created the foundation upon which later philosophies have been built. Still, while no tower can stand without a firm foundation, that doesn't mean that the many floors that have been built upon them and might be added in the future are any less important or valuable.

**Practical Takeaway**

When reading about the ancient genesis of ideas it is easy to feel distant from them. Since we've only learned about them through history, it's natural to think of them as a different species, with skin made out of pure white marble. But the ancients were humans just like we are and the lessons they taught are still being put into action by people today.

Take out your paper and writing utensil. Now, think about people who exhibit Stoic virtues. They can be people you know in real life or people you know from the media.

Stoic ideas have permeated Western culture. This means that even people who have never heard the word Stoicism have been influenced in some way by its ideas. There is also the fact that Stoicism draws from the realities of life and nature. People all across the globe have come to Stoic understanding without any connection with the ancient Greeks.

It can be hard to read about virtues in the abstract and then translate it into the real world. This is why it's helpful to look for people who personify the virtues. You shouldn't view them as divine beings, but you can use them to help guide yourself in the right direction.

The history of Stoicism isn't over, it's an ongoing process.

# Chapter 3: The Power of Perception

*You have power over your mind—not outside events. Realize this, and you will find strength.*

—Marcus Aurelius

While Stoicism is famous for the approach it takes with regards to emotions, or lack thereof, the truth is that the real power of Stoicism comes in its logical and pragmatic approach to dealing with reality.

The Stoics believed in dealing with the world as it actually exists. This might seem to be a simple-minded statement but once you come to understand what this means you'll understand the profound implications.

If you want to find a solution, you must first size up the problem with clear and objective eyes. Doing anything less will only set you up for failure.

## The Distance Between the World and Our Perception

The Stoics believed that there were three disciplines that were required to live a Stoic lifestyle. The first was perception, the second action, and the third will. This order is not an accident, there is a reason that perception is considered to be the primary discipline of Stoicism.

Perception is all about seeing the world as it actually is. It is about looking at reality as objectively as possible, taking value judgements out of the picture.

If you ask most people about how accurately they perceive the world they will tell you that they see things perfectly clear. After all, if they have two healthy eyes how else would they see things? But perception isn't just about your physical sight, it's about the way your mind processes the information you take in when you gaze out at the world.

The mind processes visual information in two steps. The first is when the light bouncing off of the object enters the eye and you perceive the reality in front of you visually. The second step is when your brain takes the image and applies a label to it. This second step is where the trouble comes in.

The problem isn't looking at a duck and calling it a duck. The trouble is that we look at tasks in front of us and we quickly jump to conclusions over whether they are possible or not. We look at people just long enough to take in their appearance and then decide whether or not we can trust them. We look at ourselves and judge what we are capable of without any solid reasoning backing up our conclusions.

Humans are driven to make judgements and our judgments are often far from the mark. This is what the Stoics understood, and it's why they put such an emphasis on correcting our perception so that we see the world as it actually is before we try and act within it.

## First Day on The Job

To help understand the destructive nature of inaccurate perception I will walk you through a scenario. Imagine that you are showing up to your first day at a new job and you are meeting with your coworkers. In this scenario you are a rather judgmental person who is prone to quickly jumping to conclusions about everyone you meet.

You walk into the office and the first person you meet is your new boss. He shakes your hand, but his grip is a little limp. You immediately label him as weak before moving onto the next person. The first coworker you meet has a smile on their face but a stain on their shirt. The word "slob" comes to mind before you leave that person to meet another. The final person you meet greets you kindly but has a monotone voice, so you can't help but think of them as boring.

Now, think about how those instantly generated labels might impact your future working relationships with those individuals. Conclusions you jumped to in this scenario based on next to no information could color your interactions with your coworkers for years to come.

Hopefully you are now beginning to see how easily our perception can become clouded by an overeagerness to judge the world around us. The untrained mind jumps to conclusions almost instantly, but the judgements it doles out can linger for days, weeks, or even years.

**Slow to Judge and Slow to Trust**

While some people may already be on board with a more objective approach to reality, I know that there will be others who are reluctant. You might have read through the "First Day on the Job" segment and felt that the character in the scenario was right to make those judgements. Often people will defend these sorts of judgements on practical grounds. There are a lot of people out there, some of them have bad intentions, and if you wait for such individuals to reveal their bad intentions before taking precautions then you will be left at their will.

This is a fair point, but it misses the point of delaying judgement. Many people assume that if you won't label someone as dishonest then you are declaring that they are honest. But this simply isn't the case. You can withhold both positive and negative judgments at the same time. If you don't know someone well, you can withhold both trust and distrust until you've gotten a chance to get a better idea of who they are as a person.

Remember that Stoicism is about engaging with the world in a rational and logical way. If you know you are entering an area where crime is common you don't have to pretend like this information is unavailable to you. If reason says that safety precautions should be taken, then by all means, take safety precautions.

Still, consider where you are getting your information from. Are you judging the risk level based on objective information or snap judgements based off of personal biases? People tend to overrate their own objectivity.

The fact is that it takes time and energy to cultivate the ability to see the world as it actually is. For most people, it's not like a switch that can be flipped on or off, even if you can withhold judgement for a while you might find yourself sliding back into old habits before too long. But there's no reason to despair. Stoicism isn't about quick and easy solutions; it's about taking the time to bring about true and lasting change.

## A Shift in Perception

*Nothing either good nor bad but thinking makes it so.*

—William Shakespeare

Once you take the time to pay attention to the way that you perceive the world and shape it with your thoughts, you will come to realize just how much power you have. The only unfortunate thing is that you may only realize this once you recognize that you have been holding yourself back from your full potential with unwarranted negative thinking.

The good news is that it's never too late to make a

change. As long as you are still drawing breath, you can take command of your thoughts and use them to reshape your world.

## Turning the World Upside Down

There is a trick in the art world for anyone who wants to draw a complex image but feels overwhelmed when they look at it. The trick is taking the image and flipping it upside down. Suddenly the person no longer feels like they are drawing an entire head, instead they see it as drawing a field of individual shapes. When you wipe words like "difficult" or "impossible" out of the picture and focus on the individual steps, you might be amazed at what you can achieve.

The same can be said for examining your life. The average person looks at the events that lay ahead of them and focuses in on anything that seems like it will be a challenge or an obstacle. Once we label them as problems they tend to grow in our minds, becoming outsized threats that loom over us and cause unwarranted stress.

But what if you could turn the image upside down? What if you could look out at what you would normally call obstacles and call them opportunities instead?

## Transforming a Cage into a Tool

The sad fact is that most people are trapped by their own perception. Years of bias and mental programming has made it difficult for them to see the world as it is. Even worse, when they look at the world, they see so many insurmountable obstacles that they feel hopelessly restrained.

They are like a person who puts on a virtual reality headset and ends up trapped in an open field. Even though no physical walls surround them they still feel restrained because of the walls they see in their head.

Learning to see the world objectively is like taking off the headset. It shows you the full range of movement available to you. But you don't have to stop there. Taking control of your perception is like reprogramming that virtual reality headset to help you find where you're going. This is the full power of mastering your perception, you can reshape the way you see the world in a way that propels you forward rather than holding you back.

**Eliminating Worry**

Mastering perception is an especially helpful tool for anyone who struggles with worry. After all, what causes worry? Most people experience this feeling after they identify potential problems in their life and allow these potential issues to haunt their mind. As long as the issue goes unaddressed it remains a worry, floating through your conscious and wreaking havoc.

The problem with worries is that there is no limit to how many you can have. You might think you could cure them by solving your problems, but once the human mind has been trained to look for potential problems it will always find more. This is why it helps to be able to retrain your brain. Once you do there is almost no limit to what you might achieve.

## *Separating Acceptance from Agreement*

Before we move on from perception, we need to discuss a related issue, acceptance. Stoicism is built around accepting the world as it is. This is tied in with perception. The idea is that in order to perceive the world as it really is you have to be prepared to accept it as it truly is. Those who feel like the world must be a certain way will find ways to distort their perception in order to try and square their beliefs with the external world. This is something that Stoicism can't accept.

Stoicism says that any philosophy that doesn't rest on a foundation of actual reality is like a house built on sand. No matter how sturdy it may look, the lack of a solid foundation will doom it in the end.

This is why true Stoics must accept the world as it is. Doing anything else would endanger your perception and threaten everything else that comes down the line. However, it's worth noting that acceptance does not mean agreement.

## The Case for Stoic Action

It's easy to fall into the trap of thinking that Stoicism is a defeatist philosophy. The idea of a Stoic who accepts fate can conjure up an image of surrendering to the powers that be, allowing other people to take control and heading off into the mountains to meditate while the world burns. But this couldn't be further from the truth.

One of the reasons it's important to study Marcus Aurelius is because he wasn't just a great thinker, he was a man of action. He embodied the Stoic practice of acceptance while acting as the emperor of the ancient world's preeminent superpower. He didn't just stand by and accept it when the Gauls attacked Rome, he led his forces out and battled.

This leaves us with a question, was Marcus a hypocrite when he shaped the future for him and his people? Are Stoics being hypocrites when they rail against some elements of human nature while promoting others? The answer is a resounding "no!"

## Understanding the Reason Behind the Mantra

The Stoics continually point out the things that individuals cannot change in order to emphasize the things that they can. The "fate" that is to be accepted isn't everything in reality, it's everything beyond our own sphere of influence.

This sphere's core is our own behavior, the one thing in life that we have anywhere near total control. Beyond that, we have the people and things around us that we can interact with. This is an area where we have some influence, but we don't ultimately have control in the same way that have control over our own thoughts and actions. Beyond this second layer is the rest of the universe, which is completely within the hands of fate.

Take a moment to think about this. There are over 6 billion people on this planet. How many do you know or interact with on a regular basis? Even if you regularly interact with thousands of people, that's still less than one percent of one percent of the world's population. In the grand scheme of things, most human activity is beyond our ability to control or even influence in any real way. But does that mean that it isn't worth trying?

Stoicism isn't just about self-help. It's a philosophy oriented around virtue, and virtue has always been understood to be a community project. The person who lives alone on a desert island rarely gets a chance to display the sort of virtues that someone in a community can practice every day.

So, while Stoicism asks that you accept the world as it exists at this point in time, it doesn't mean that the world must always remain the way it is. On the contrary, Stoics understand that the only real constant is change. The world is in flux and you as an individual are compelled to act in a virtuous manner, for the sake of yourself, your community, and your world.

Stoics have brought about real change throughout history and there's no reason for this trend to stop with you. The beauty of Stoicism is that once you stop to gain control of your own mind you can achieve levels of efficacy that you might never have dreamed about before. Thoughtless flailing is replaced with carefully considered action. Emotionalism is traded in for a logical commitment to your cause.

And finally, the obstacles that once held you back can be transformed. Events that seemed like problems become opportunities, helping you chart a course into the future that you never would have thought possible without Stoic thinking.

Careful thought can allow you to stop worrying about circumstances that are beyond your control and focus in on those that are within your ability to command. You can stop wasting time, energy, and resources on pointless worry and start becoming a more effective and fulfilled human being. This sort of transformation isn't quick or easy, but it can improve your life immeasurably if you're willing to commit to it.

So, you see, Stoics may have to accept the current reality but that doesn't mean they have to agree with it. They are free to work to bring about change, and the skills developed by practicing Stoicism actually make it easier to achieve real results in this world.

**Practical Takeaway**

Using your powers of perception to turn obstacles into opportunities is one of the most powerful weapons in a Stoic's arsenal. If you want to master this ability, then you should start practicing as soon as possible.

Take out your paper and writing utensil. Now, take the time and write down an obstacle or problem you have been worrying about lately.

Once you have finished writing the problem down, take another moment to reexamine the situation you are dealing with more objectively. Describe it in cold and technical terms, avoiding emotion or any other powerful language.

Now take things one step further and consider how the objective situation you are dealing with might offer some hidden opportunity.

If you have gone through these steps, then you will have taken a source of worry in your life and turned it into an opportunity to develop as a human being. This is a process you can use time and time again throughout your day. There is no telling how many opportunities you might uncover if you learn how to master your perception.

# Chapter 4: Healthy and Unhealthy Passions

*He who reigns within himself, and rules passions, desires, and fears, is more than a king.*

—John Milton

Some people who stumble upon Stoicism hear that it is about accepting the external world and taking control of your own mind and assume that it is a simple endeavor. They then look inward and discover that the world inside of them is in a state that is as chaotic as the external world.

Human beings are complex creatures. We only think that we are simple when we don't take the time to truly examine our own mental lives. Every moment we are a jumble of conscious and subconscious thoughts, all charged with powerful emotions. To make matters worse, all of these thoughts and emotions can be highly contradictory, clashing and transforming from moment to moment as we make our way through life.

Accepting the fact that we aren't in control of the world is difficult, but it's not half as hard as actually gaining some semblance of control over our own interior life. But the Stoics didn't shy away from this challenge, they charted a course that each one of us can take towards mastering our own passions and regaining control of our lives.

## Examining the Passions

As you can see by now, stoicism is very interested in the internal life. The way we think and feel is one of the first things that we need to address because everything flows from them. If you never learn to control your emotions then you will be controlled by them.

One interesting thing about the Stoics' approach is that they devised a plan for enlightenment that didn't call for completely jettisoning emotions. They categorized what we would call emotions into two categories, pathe, or unhealthy passions, and eupatheiai, or healthy thoughts. These categories were established by Zeno and carried forward by future Stoics.

We'll start with the unhealthy passions:

- **Pain**
    - This passion is defined as the feeling you get when experiencing something inaccurately labeled as bad. It's the emotion we feel when we linger on injuries, insults, or any other perceived misfortune that we experience. This passion causes us to suffer unnecessarily because of our

perceptions rather than reality.

- **Fear**
  - This is the irrational drive to avoid problems that we might expect. Pay attention to the word "irrational." This is the impulse that shows us dangers lurking in every shadow even when we know that there is almost certainly nothing to fear. This passion wastes our time and energy on imaginary threats when we should be focusing on real problems.

- **Craving**
  - This is the irrational urge to seek after something that is mistakenly understood as good. Once again, the key words here are "irrational" and "mistakenly." The problem isn't desire, the issue is that the thing being desired isn't actually the good that the seeker believes it to be. Stoics are concerned that life is wasted on craving after things of no real value when it should be spent seeking after things that are right and virtuous.

- **Pleasure**
  - This is the irrational feeling of euphoria that is experienced when a person chooses something that isn't virtuous or worthwhile. This is the seductive nature of sin and misbehavior

manifested emotionally. Pleasure is a feeling that leads people astray from the path of virtue, feeling good in the moment but leading to guilt and suffering in the long term.

If this all sounds like a guilt trip, don't worry. Stoicism isn't a legalistic philosophy that is all about punishing people who violate its strict rules. These descriptions might sound harsh, but you need to remember that Stoics believe that these passions are unhealthy and destructive.

The point isn't that some Stoic sage will punish you if you feel these passions, it's that these passions will lead you down a destructive road. In Stoicism, you end up punishing yourself when you don't act in line with virtue. But on the other hand, you can save yourself from your darker impulses by learning to practice healthy thinking.

With that in mind, let's look at the healthy thoughts:

- **Caution**
    - The logical impulse to avoid actions that violate virtue. This healthy thought can be understood as the drive to avoid harming others, to keep away from negative influences, and to avert any course of action that would violate your personal values.

- **Wishing**
    - This is the proper desire for virtuous action or results. The desire to do right

by others, to protect the innocent, and to live according to your personal values can all be categorized as wishing. Stoicism would say that when you feel your conscious guiding you towards a certain course of virtuous action you are experiencing the healthy thought of wishing.

- **Joy**
    - This is defined as a rational happiness brought about by virtuous actions or events. The life of a Stoic isn't gray and cheerless, the idea is that the Stoic rejoices in everything that is truly good. When a Stoic chooses to take a course of action that is in line with their values then they can feel joy in their achievement and the good results that it might have brought about.

This system of categorization can be a little confusing at first. The English labels used can often feel very blurry since they aren't quite as distinct as the ancient Greek words that the original Stoics used. But what shouldn't be too hard to understand is the idea that everything revolves around virtue.

The unhealthy passions are almost all oriented towards pulling you to violate virtue or your personal values, while the healthy thoughts are all about pushing you in the direction of virtuous living. Understanding this is the most important takeaway, if you can do this then the more subtle distinctions will become clear with further study.

**Opposing Passions**

One of the brilliant things about this categorization is the way that unhealthy passions are paired with healthy thoughts. Fear is paired with caution, craving is paired with wishing, and pleasure is paired with joy. Instead of seeing each of the six emotions as being completely distinct and separate from the rest, you can view them as three continuums with a healthy side and an unhealthy side. This means that it's not about getting rid of certain emotions but moving along a spectrum to a healthier way of thinking.

For example, pleasure is the opposite of joy. This means that if you want to live a healthier life you need to take the part of yourself that is constantly seeking after pleasure and redirect it to seek joy.

To clarify even further, imagine you are on a diet. Losing weight and becoming healthier are values to you, so you want to take actions that are in line with these values. You wake up in the morning, head to the office, and find two breakfast snacks are on the table, a donut and an apple. Which do you take?

Your pleasure drive is the side pushing you towards the donut. Stoics see pleasure as an enjoyable feeling that ultimately works against your values. In this case the donut will prevent you from achieving your goals. So, while it feels "good" in the moment it is ultimately a self-destructive feeling. On the other hand, eating the apple would give you joy because it is in line with your goal. It is a thoroughly good feeling, something that points you toward virtue rather than away from it.

Stoicism says that you don't have to wallow in denial. You can spend all day moping over the fact that you didn't get the donut you want, or you can take joy in the fact that you made a healthy choice and are now living in line with your values. The idea is that you shouldn't allow unhealthy passions to control or monopolize your mind. By emphasizing and dwelling on healthy thoughts you can gain more control over your life and live with greater calmness and contentment.

### The Unique Problem of Pain

You might have noticed that when we were discussing the emotional pairs created by the stoics, we didn't mention pain. That is because the stoics believed that pain was a unique passion that had no healthy parallel. So, while the stoics sought to transform most passions, they were trying to rid themselves of the passion of pain.

Notice that I am specifying that we are talking about a passion here. When Stoics talk about eliminating pain or suffering, they are not talking about removing them as physical sensations. If you punch any stoic, they will feel pain, stoicism can unlock many doors, but it won't make you superhuman. The difference comes in how the stoic reacts mentally to being punched.

The Stoics defined the passion of pain as a "failure to avoid something mistakenly judged bad" (Internet Encyclopedia of Philosophy). Notice the words "judged bad."

For a stoic, avoiding pain is all about changing your perception. Things you don't want to happen are going to happen to you. There is nothing you can do to fully protect yourself. What you can do is change the way you think about the things that happen. You can jump to labeling them as bad and fall into a cycle of suffering or you can train yourself to accept the things that happen and transcend suffering.

**One Injury, Two Pains**

Stoicism says that when we are injured, we actually feel two types of pain. The first type of pain is the physical sensation of pain that is our body's natural warning system to alert us that something isn't right. This type of pain is part of nature and an important part of life. There are people who don't feel pain and these individuals are more likely to suffer permanent injuries because they don't have pain to act as a warning sign to get them to back off. Stoics are against the second instance of pain, which is the pain we feel as we dwell on the initial injury and wallow in our emotional reaction.

This is true for both physical injuries and emotional injuries. Think about the times when you have been insulted. The first suffering you felt was the almost automatic sting of being attacked and then you felt the prolonged suffering of dealing with the aftermath of the insult. Take a moment to think about insults you can still remember, and you might be surprised to realize how far back your mind can recall even minor slights.

Human beings have a way of holding onto pain. We might argue that we need to, because if we were to quickly let go of and forget painful events then we might not learn from them. But Stoicism argues that you can learn from insults and injuries without dwelling on them. In fact, it argues that true learning requires a level of detachment that we don't feel when we hold onto our suffering.

How many arguments escalate into feuds because neither side is willing to let go of their pain? How many minor slights lead to destructive schisms because people like to dwell on problems until they grow out of proportion?

Stoicism looks at emotional pain like a physical cut. If you want a cut to heal then you need to leave it alone. If you keep picking at your wound it won't scab over and heal. This goes for physical and emotional wounds. Dwelling on insults and injuries may feel like the right thing to do, but it is actually a highly destructive course of action.

**No Flip Side**

If you can recall the first section of this chapter, where we first introduced the various passions, then you'll remember that most of the unhealthy passions were linked with healthy thoughts. The only passion that didn't have such a link was pain.

This is because Stoics believed that pain was a unique passion. The idea is that the passion of pain is entirely irrational and therefore there is no rational way to process this emotion. This is a case where the goal is total elimination.

You could say that the opposite of pain is acceptance. Pain or suffering is what you feel when you struggle against the world as it is. When the rain is falling on you and you say to yourself "this is an awful situation," then you are putting yourself through pain. The solution is to stop applying the label. Simply say to yourself "rain is falling upon me." You don't need to try and trick yourself into believing that something good is happening to you, the idea is that you simply stop thinking that you are suffering and then the suffering will cease.

**Transcending Suffering**

One of the ultimate goals of Stoicism is to move beyond suffering. You could even say that Stoicism was created in response to the uniquely human problem of suffering.

I say "uniquely human" because as far as we can tell at this point and time, humans are the only creatures on Earth that can suffer in the sense that Stoicism is concerned with. Once again, this doesn't mean that the many animals on this earth don't feel physical pain or agony when they are harmed. What I'm talking about is the suffering that we inflict upon ourselves when we dwell on the circumstances, we believe to be negative.

We can't stop others from harming us, but we can work to ensure that we don't inflict unnecessary harm upon ourselves. So many people are their own worst enemies, taking momentary issues and stretching them out across their entire lives. Pain that could be gone in a matter of moments becomes a permanent companion.

It's time to reject pain. Feel what you have to feel and then move on with your life. It might sound impossible, but you will be able to discover the things your mind can do if you are willing to take the time to develop your skills and take command of your thoughts. Physical pain may always be a fact of life, but with practice you can dramatically cut down on the mental pain that you put yourself through.

### Striking a Balance

Striking an emotional balance can seem like a difficult process. After all, how does one even start? Thankfully Stoicism has a solution. The answer is virtue.

One of the big struggles that comes with addressing problems related to our interior lives is the risk of getting lost inside of ourselves. The human mind can be a labyrinth of contradictions and the heart can be even more vexing. Introspection is difficult for many people, while others find it so addictive that they get lost within themselves. Believe it or not, when we search within ourselves it can be all too easy to get lost. That's why it's helpful to have something beyond ourselves that we can use as a guide.

This is where virtue comes in. Virtue is that which orients all Stoic pursuit. The Stoics didn't believe that self-improvement was a materialist pursuit that was all about making more money, gaining more prestige, or simply feeling better about oneself. The Stoics believed that life had a purpose and that was to live a virtuous life.

This is especially important when it comes to our emotions or passions. If your emotions are oriented towards virtue and your personal values, then you will have a healthy emotional life. But if your emotions are constantly leading you away from virtue and towards vice then your emotions will continually lead you into pain and frustration.

**Developing a Healthy Emotional Life**

Stoicism is all about getting your mind under control, and that means getting a grip on your emotions. If your emotions are driving you, then you aren't in true control of your life, which is the only thing that Stoics believe you can truly control. This is why emotions are so important to Stoics.

You might believe that your emotions aren't under your control, but this is a colossal error. You may never have asked for the emotions that you feel, but that doesn't mean that you are powerless to the influence of your emotions.

It might be true that you don't control the emotions that you feel, but you can choose how you react to the different emotions as they arise. Through hard work and dedication, you can empower your positive and constructive emotions while downplaying your negative and destructive emotions.

There is a chance that you will be able to get your emotions under control by sheer force of will, but don't be afraid to seek help if you feel like you need it. Getting help from friends, support groups, or trained professionals can be very beneficial to this process. Remember, being a Stoic doesn't mean that you can't ask for help. Sometimes the bravest thing you can do is reach out to someone else.

**Practical Takeaway**

Stoicism is all about mastering your passions by identifying problem areas and working to turn them around. With that in mind, it's time to dig down deep to find a passion that you are struggling with.

Take out your writing utensil and paper. Now, write down a passion that you struggle with, aside from pain.

Remember, you're looking for an emotion that is destructive. It's something that is leading you away from the virtuous life you want to live.

Now that you have an unhealthy passion written down, go back to the start of this chapter and find a healthy thought that corresponds to the passion you chose. Write it down across from the unhealthy passion.

Now, consider how you can help yourself move away

from your unhealthy passion and toward a healthier thought pattern. The idea is that you don't need to give up on your emotions, you simply need to redirect them in a healthier and more productive direction.

This process won't instantly transform your thoughts, but it will help you become more aware of your issues and point you toward a potential solution. Remember, you can't address a problem until you identify it. Ignoring your issues allows them to fester and grow out of control. Addressing them head on is the only way to regain command of your mind and control of your life.

# Chapter 5: Taking Action

*Don't explain your philosophy. Embody it.*

—Epictetus

The world is filled with people who take no action and then sit around wondering why nothing is going according to their wishes. They lament what has happened in the past, fret about what will happen in the future, and remain passive in the present.

Stoics reject this approach. While they practice acceptance, it doesn't mean they are passive. They accept the world around them that they cannot control. This allows for a greater focus on what can be controlled, your own actions.

## No More Armchair Philosophers

What does a philosopher look like to you?

For many people, the word philosopher conjures up an image of an old white guy wearing a tweed jacket, sitting in an overstuffed armchair thinking intently about something very serious.

What you need to understand is that philosophy isn't just for people who can make money writing or talking about its study, philosophy is for everyone.

Just about every thinking person on this earth has a philosophy, the problem is that most people come upon their philosophies unthinkingly.

Many people act without really understanding the ideas and beliefs driving their actions. And many philosophers think very deeply about ideas and beliefs but rarely take action based on their conclusions. The stoic considers both of these paths as tragic. Stoicism was developed to be lived, not just studied.

This is probably one of the reasons why the history of stoicism is filled with so many philosophers who achieved amazing things outside of the realm of pure thought. It's a philosophy by people who took action, for people who want to take action.

It's often been said that one of the big problems with this world is that the people who take action don't think about what they are doing while the people who think about what they are doing never end up taking action. This line might be a bit of an exaggeration, but it does get at a valuable truth. The world needs more people who are able to marry thought and action together to create the sort of meaningful change that we long for as a society.

**What Action Means**

In this book we'll be talking a lot about action, but this is a word that is easy to misunderstand. When most modern people think of a person of action they picture someone who is in constant motion. Someone who has a packed schedule filled with very impressive activities. But this isn't the sort of action we're talking about.

Deciding to stop for a moment and take a deep breath before continuing is an action. Holding a defensive position rather than going on the attack is an action. Keeping your eyes closed and your body still can be an action. What matters is intentionality. You need to think about what you're doing and then take a course of action that is in line with your thinking.

Action is something you actively and consciously choose to do. Reaction is something you do passively or subconsciously.

Laying down in bed because you want to get a full night's rest is taking action. Laying down in bed because you have so many things to do that you feel overwhelmed is a reaction. Deciding to do nothing when someone cusses you out because you don't want to escalate the situation is taking action. Lashing out and attacking that person and making the situation worse is a reaction.

Many people in this world seem like they have a lot going on, but they are actually living reactively. They move unthinkingly from one action to the next until they lay down to go to sleep and forget everything they did that day. Meanwhile, some people who look lazy by mainstream standards may be living a life of constant, deliberate action that is aligned with their goals and values.

If your goal is to clear your mind, then your best course of action might be heading out into nature and experiencing peace and quiet. If you want to understand yourself, then you might meditate in a dark and silent room. If you want to get closer with your family, then you might spend a day just hanging out and playing with them.

In a modern consumerist society it's easy to fall into the trap of thinking that the only actions that have value are those that produce tangible results. We always want something to "show for our efforts." Even hobbies that are supposed to be relaxing, like video games, quickly become competitions to rack up points, earn achievements, and compare ourselves with others.

So, while a stoic should take action, they take action based on stoic values. They don't move to impress others, they move as an expression of their core values. They don't ask "how will this look to other people?" They ask "how will this help me develop my virtue?"

As you look at your life and the lives of those around you, be sure that you don't mistake movement for action. Some of the most active souls are the most unassuming, while some of the emptiest lives are booked solid with meaningless activities. Don't allow frivolous distractions to keep you from the meaningful actions you need to undertake.

**The True Value of Action**

Finally, it's worth explaining why action is so important to Stoics. It isn't just because Stoicism was developed by practical individuals, although this is certainly part of it. The deeper reason is that Stoics believe the entire meaning of life is the development of our personal virtues and the creation of a more virtuous world. This is a goal that can't be achieved without action.

If you want to become a calmer, more controlled, and more virtuous individual, then you will need to take action. You won't achieve these sorts of lofty goals by reading about other people, you need to plot a course of action and follow it yourself.

This is the path that Stoics have taken for thousands of years and it's the path that is open to you. The question is whether or not you are willing to do what it takes to become the person you want to be.

## *Overcoming Analysis Paralysis*

One of the biggest issues that holds thoughtful people back from taking action is a phenomenon known as analysis paralysis. This label was invented to describe the all too common scenario where someone becomes bogged down in considering all the possible options available or all the conceivable angles, to the point that they become unable to commit to any particular course of action.

This phenomenon is especially common with the sort of people who are interested in subjects like philosophy. Introspective and analytic individuals are very good at seeing the different sides of issues, which is a fantastic thing until it becomes a negative thing. You should always strive to think your actions through, but at a certain point you need to act.

We live in a world that is overflowing with choice. It can feel like every moment of every day is filled with countless choices. How are we supposed to take action when it feels like it's impossible to choose which of the thousands of paths available to us is the best?

Thankfully, Stoicism has some helpful tips for cutting through the chaos and charting a path forward. It won't provide you with the answers to every question you face but it will give you some tools that will help you to make decisions that will move your life forward in a positive and productive manner.

**Moving Virtuously**

Once again we must return to that key Stoic concept: virtue. This is an especially important thing to consider when we talk about action since our actions usually have consequences that reach beyond ourselves.

Stoicism says that when we plot a course of action the most important consideration is whether or not that action is virtuous. The other question is whether or not the action will help you to develop your virtue.

If you want to live a life according to Stoic principles then one of the most important things to do is come to some understanding of what virtue means to you. You can read books about what virtue is and listen to debates between proponents of different ethical systems, but in the end only you can decide what you truly believe in.

It can take a long time and a lot of wrestling to develop a system of firm beliefs about what a virtuous life looks like. But once you have a firm idea in your head then you'll always be able to compare potential actions with your ideal life and ask whether or not they are in alignment. This one test can help you cut through a lot of life's clutter and move from a life of indecision and regret to a life of action and fulfillment.

Of course, not every course of action is heavy with ethical weight. When you're at the store and trying to pick a fruit to purchase, you don't have to feel as if your virtue is on the line. But that doesn't mean Stoicism has nothing to offer in these situations. When you are faced with a situation where virtue isn't at stake and you can't tell which option is preferable, then just pick an option and move on with your life.

**Dealing with Unforeseen Consequences**

I know that there are still some of you who are concerned about taking action. You might worry that even if you act with the best of intentions your actions might have unintended consequences that hurt other people. They might then get angry at you or you might have to live with the guilt for the rest of your life.

Stoicism has an answer for this. The ethical system Stoicism is based upon is virtue ethics. The idea of virtue ethics is that actions are right or wrong based on the intent of the person acting rather than the outcome of their actions. Compare this with consequentialism, which says that actions are right or wrong based on the outcome of actions rather than the intention of the people acting.

The debate between these two schools of thought has been raging for thousands of years. Good people hold to both systems of beliefs, but Stoics have a good reason for falling where they do. One of the most fundamental principles of Stoicism is that we only control our own thoughts and actions, we cannot control the outcome of our actions. If you believe this then it doesn't make sense to get bent out of shape worrying about unexpected consequences since they are by definition impossible to predict.

Please note that this doesn't mean you should act without thinking things through. Stoics still do their due diligence to ensure that their actions don't have consequences that aren't readily apparent but could be predicted based on an examination of all of the evidence. The idea is simply that at some point things are beyond our ability to predict. You can't blame others for the unpredictable consequences of their actions and you shouldn't feel guilt over the same sort of results.

All of this is easier said than done. Even with knowing these things, it can still be painful to watch as plans go awry and people suffer because of your well-intended decisions. But a Stoic seeks to transcend this suffering, understanding that it has no value. Nothing is improved when you beat yourself up over things you can't control, your pain will never heal others. This is why the Stoic doesn't dwell on unfortunate circumstances, they only seek to learn what they can and move forward.

## What's the Worst That Can Happen?

Another way to encourage yourself to take action is by stopping to consider what is really keeping you from moving. One of the most common ways that people get in their own way is by dwelling on the worst case scenarios that may result from their choices. While I could suggest that you should just ignore these scenarios because they're almost always highly unlikely, in this case I'm going to suggest that you face them head on.

So, take a second and consider what might realistically be the worst possible outcome of the choice you're considering. Now that you have this scenario in mind, ask yourself whether or not you'd be able to live with the consequences.

The fact of the matter is that humans are more durable than we often give ourselves credit for. We can survive great injuries, both literal and metaphorical. Every day people suffer tragedies and every day people go on living with the aftermath.

Now, take a second to consider the actual odds that you'll end up dealing with a true worst-case scenario. Unless you're a daredevil or considering something that is uncommonly dangerous, then you're probably going to walk away from the aftermath of a failed attempt without much trouble.

Of course, there are some situations where the consequences can be deadly. And in these cases it's worth remembering that we are all going to die at some point. This doesn't mean that you should throw your life away, but it does mean that you should fool yourself into thinking that by avoiding potentially deadly risks you can live forever. You can live inside a bubble your entire life, doing nothing but exercising and eating healthy food, and in the end you'll still die.

Please understand that I am not suggesting that you take risks for the sake of taking risks. That's not the Stoic way. The idea isn't to seek out troubles and misfortune, it's to recognize that we don't really need to be afraid of the things that keep us up at night. No one wants to deal with failure, but failure isn't the end of the world. The truth is that success can lead to failure and failure can lead to success. That's why a Stoic takes life as it comes, making the best out of every situation.

### *Moving Swiftly and Boldly*

Remember the most basic concept of Stoicism: life is what you make of it. What other people might see as setbacks or disappointments; a Stoic can see as opportunities. When you live with a Stoic mindset you don't have to live in fear. You can make decisions with complete confidence since you know that no matter what happens you'll be able to handle the outcome. As long as you are making your decisions with an eye towards virtue, then you can live without regrets.

## Every Outcome is an Opportunity

The other thing to consider when looking at action through a Stoic lens is that no matter whether an action leads to a "failure" or a "success," the outcome is more properly seen as an opportunity. A true Stoic rejects labels like "failure" and "success" for this reason. They would say that life is a series of situations where we have an opportunity to develop our virtues.

Success gives you an opportunity to develop your humility and generosity, keeping your head on your shoulders and sharing the wealth with those around you. Meanwhile, failure allows you to develop the virtues of perseverance and creativity. It's easy to keep going when everything goes according to plan, it takes real character to keep moving and coming up with new plans in spite of your previous failures.

American history wouldn't be the same if General Ulysses S. Grant had always gotten his wish. Unlike many of history's greatest leaders, Grant was a humble man. When he attended West Point, his dream wasn't to become a general, he only hoped that he could become a math teacher and earn a living for himself and his beloved Julia.

Still, he felt an obligation to the military that had paid for his education and followed its orders as it led him into Mexico, across Panama, and over to the far frontier of California. When Grant saw San Francisco he felt a new calling in life and dreamed of moving to the city someday. But life away from his family hit him hard and he took to drinking. He ended up being discharged from the Army under a shadow of shame that would follow him his entire life (Largay, 2014).

For ten years he would struggle to eke out a living back East, left to wallow in shame over the failure of his military career. But what he didn't know was that the fast-approaching American Civil War would allow him to quickly climb the ranks of the Union Army and become the most powerful American General since George Washington.

Grant wouldn't just see his own fortune turn around; he would change the fortune of a nation. He was Abraham Lincoln's last hope, replacing a long series of generals who had failed to defeat Robert E. Lee. By the time Grant took power, the Union enjoyed many advantages over the Confederates on paper, but the population was sick and tired of war. Lincoln was up for reelection and it looked like he would lose to a candidate who would sue for peace with the South, allowing the rebellious states to finally break away from the Union and secure the future of slavery in America.

If Grant had gotten his wish and become a college professor, he never would have gotten the military experience that would prepare him for the Civil War. If he had been able to succeed on the West Coast and settle down in San Francisco, then he almost certainly would have been left there to defend the territory from foreign attack during the Civil War.

If Grant hadn't failed miserably time and time again in his life, he never would have been able to become the legend he is today. Going farther, it's very possible that Grant's personal failures ultimately saved the Union and freed countless men and women from the bondage of slavery.

## Success Grows from the Field of Failure

The case of Ulysses S. Grant is rather extreme, but the basic pattern is something that can be seen in every walk of life. If you read the biography of almost any successful individual, you'll see that they wouldn't have achieved what they did if they hadn't failed at some point in their life. Failures that seemed insurmountable at the time would ultimately pave the way to previously unimaginable successes.

No one is born with their perfect life mapped out before them. Believe it or not, succeeding in the first thing you try is not necessarily the path to happiness. Sometimes failure is necessary to point you in a direction where you will be happier and more fulfilled.

When you stop focusing on viewing life through the binary lens of success and failure, you'll be able to see that everything is an opportunity. This can help free you from your paralysis. Instead of waiting and waiting for a perfect opportunity that might never come you can allow yourself to move forward with confidence, knowing that the sooner you take action the sooner you'll find new opportunities.

Fortune favors the bold. The perfect opportunity isn't just going to fall into your lap, it will only reveal itself if you put yourself out there and keep looking for chances where others aren't looking.

**Practical Takeaway**

For this chapter you're going to be asked to do something a little different.

Put your paper and writing utensils to the side. Now think about what you need to do right this moment. Chances are you are putting something off that you could do right now. It might be something big for your work or it might be something small like taking out the garbage or sending a quick message to someone you've been meaning to talk to. Or it might be something internal, like taking some time to silently meditate.

Do you have something in mind? Do it right now.

Alright, did you get it done? Hopefully you did, but I know there are some good excuses why you might have just kept reading. You might be on a crowded bus, or sitting on a beach, or in some other situations where you can't do the thing you need to do or where you have no real obligations. You still could have taken a minute for silent meditation, but we'll just move on.

If you're in one of these situations and are just reading through the book without doing this or any of the other assignments, don't beat yourself up over it. But you should understand that the benefits you see will be diminished. So, I would recommend that you try and do these practical assignments as soon as you are able to.

Humans are naturally lazy creatures. We will grab onto any excuse that allows us to shirk our duties. The only way to overcome this natural tendency towards inaction is by deliberately developing a habit of taking action. It might be tough in the beginning, but it's necessary if you want to reach your full potential.

# Chapter 6: Viewing the World Through a Stoic Lens

*We must take a higher view of all things, and bear with them more easily: it better becomes a man to scoff at life than to lament over it.*

—Seneca

While Stoicism starts with looking inward, eventually the Stoic needs to look out at the world around them. Control starts with understanding your own emotions, but eventually you need to consider how you fit in with the world around you.

Every philosophy tries to make sense of the chaotic and confusing world and stoicism isn't any different. It offers people a true worldview, a way to look at the world around you and make sense of what it is happening. When you truly understand stoic concepts, you'll be able to make sense of many of the things that previously vexed you. This doesn't mean that the actions of others will suddenly become logical, but you'll be able to understand the sort of errors that lead to the messes you see whenever you turn on the television or open a newspaper.

# Neither Pessimism nor Optimism

"Are you a pessimist or an optimist?"

This is the sort of question that people love to ask. It appeals to our natural desire to divide the world into black and white extremes that we can quickly and easily label for our own purposes.

Stoicism falls outside this binary way of seeing the world. While some people might think that Stoicism sounds pessimistic, the truth is that it rejects the extremes of both pessimism and optimism.

Look at it this way: an optimist looks at a glass of water and says it's half full. A pessimist looks at a glass of water and says it's half empty. A Stoic looks at a glass of water an accepts whatever amount of water is in the glass.

Remember, Stoicism is all about accepting the world as it is since it is beyond our control. We have some control over our future when we take command of our own actions, but we still can't control how people and things will react to our actions and the butterfly effect that our choices might create.

The other thing to remember is that Stoicism is about transcending labels like good and bad. An optimist expects that good things will happen, a pessimist expects bad things to happen, while a Stoic expects things to happen.

## No Expectations

One thing that a Stoic should avoid is confident expectations about what will happen in the future. This is because the Stoic understands that the only thing, they control is themselves. The world is filled with forces beyond our control. We can seek to understand and influence these forces, but even at our most powerful we are severely limited.

So many people believe that their life should be like a symphony, where all the notes are perfectly laid out in front of them and all they need to do is play along and everything will work out just fine. The Stoic understands that this is folly.

Stoicism tells us that life is more like a jazz concert. Patterns may arise from time to time, but they are constantly changing, and it is up to us to improvise along and try and create something beautiful out of the chaos that surrounds us. The moment you think you know the tune and can turn your mind off is the instant when the tempo will change, and you will be left behind.

For some people this is a supremely frustrating revelation. They will struggle to hold onto their old way of thinking even as the world constantly violates their beliefs and confounds their thinking. An unfortunate amount of people experiences lives of frustration because they can never understand this fact.

Those who succeed are those who embrace reality as it is, chaos and all. Even if it isn't the way that you'd prefer things to be you can still find beauty if you know where to look. When life isn't laid out perfectly in front of you it's possible to experience the feeling of freedom in the moment, using every opportunity you find to seek out self-improvement and fulfillment.

Viewed through this lens, the world of Stoicism doesn't look so dreary. I believe you will find that many Stoic beliefs that seem somber or dark at first glance actually prove to be uplifting and life-affirming if you take the time to properly understand them.

### *Reading Beyond the Headlines*

As you learn to see the world through a Stoic lens you will come to understand how few people take this approach. Very few human beings seek to transcend their emotions, allowing passion to cloud their vision and control the actions that they take.

Nowhere is this clearer than when you look to the modern media. Whether you're looking at the newspaper, the television, the movie screen, or the internet, it can feel like everything is designed to make you angry, depressed, or self-conscious.

Human beings are prone to negative passions by our very nature. Those in the media understand that the easiest way to get us to engage with their products is by enflaming these passions. This is why Stoics need to be on their guard when dealing with the media.

Not all media is bad, but you must understand that most media is more interested in cranking up your passion than it is in encouraging the cultivation of personal virtue.

If you want to improve your own state of mind and live in line with Stoic virtues, then you absolutely must take time to reconsider your media diet.

## Mass Media Spin

Have you ever asked yourself what the point of media is? Is it to entertain? Is it to inform? Is it to produce work of great value? It certainly can be all of these things, but in this age of consumerism you need to remember that the most important thing any piece of media has to do is make money.

This is something most people know intellectually, but it's still easy to forget when you are watching a professionally produced piece of content that has been crafted using huge piles of cash to bypass your defenses so that you are open to whatever it has to sell.

One of the most fraught sectors of modern media is the news. This is because we can all agree that a healthy news industry is important to keep the public informed and check the ambitions of those who would manipulate and abuse the population. But you can't forget that many modern news products are as much entertainment as they are information, blurring the lines so that it becomes difficult to know when you are being informed and when you are being manipulated.

"If it bleeds, it leads." This adage is something that every Stoic should keep in mind. If you turn on the news on any given day, you're likely to find yourself dealing with a deluge of death, destruction, and horror that can be difficult to stomach.

With all of the horror parading across our screens at every hour of the day it can be easy to believe that we are living in one of the worst periods of human history. But if you take the time to compare statistics about the modern world with those from just a few decades ago, you'll see a much different picture.

By many measures, we are actually living in one of the most healthy, safe, and prosperous periods in recorded history. Please understand that I'm not suggesting that those who point out real suffering in this world are doing a disservice. The news should highlight injustice and bring it to the attention of people who might be able to make a change. But in a world that is packed with more than six billion souls, there will never be any end to sob stories.

When you watch the news or take in the media, please remember that it isn't necessarily painting an accurate image of life. Acts of violence will always make the front page, while acts of kindness are usually relegated to the back. The people who create the media understand that it's easier to make money off of your unhealthy passions than it is to appeal to your healthier thoughts.

This is why Stoics should always look past the headlines. Don't jump to conclusions or overgeneralize from a limited amount of information. You should view the time you spend watching or reading the news as an opportunity to practice your stoic virtues, working to hold off on applying labels as you search for the deeper truth.

This isn't an easy way to consume media, but it is a healthier and more virtuous way to do it. Remember, every moment of your life is an opportunity to develop your virtue, whether you're with friends or sitting at home and scrolling through your phone. The true Stoic is constantly vigilant for opportunities to develop and grow.

**Social Media Sickness**

While traditional media has always played upon human passions, the latest media innovation has taken this approach to a whole new level. Social media is a more potent and addictive version of the old mass media. It's true that social media can do many wonderful things, but it can also have a wide range of destructive side effects that too many people are unaware of.

Social media sites like Facebook, Twitter, and Instagram are designed to tap into your subconscious to create a sense of dependency. They draw you in by claiming that they foster community and then get you hooked on the dopamine rush that you get when people "like" the content you share.

None of this is to say that you have to delete your social media accounts. For better or for worse, social media sites have become important places for gathering information, connecting with peers, and doing business. With all of this in mind, you may have plenty of good reasons why you can't simply abandon social media. But that doesn't mean that you can't rethink the way that you use these sites.

By cutting back or rethinking the way that you use social media, you can mitigate its negative impact while doubling down on the more positive aspects. This is a difficult needle to thread, but if you want to live a happier and healthier life, it's worth thinking critically and carefully about the role that social media plays in your daily routine.

## Unplugging from the Matrix

The business of manipulating the unhealthy passions of human beings is a billion-dollar business. Advertising, entertainment, news, politics, all of these fields are run by professionals who are trained in the art of manipulating human passions in order to achieve certain goals. Some goals are more virtuous than others, but in the end the common thread connecting them all is still their manipulative nature.

Even when you understand that you are being manipulated you will likely find that it is hard to escape the traps that have been laid for you. This is the insidious genius of modern media manipulation, even people who understand that social media is making them depressed keep coming back day after day because of their personal dependency and the global web of peer pressure that surrounds them.

Please understand that I am not saying that you need

to become a luddite who forsakes all forms of technology and media to live a life of silent meditation in a monastery. Even if this would be the healthiest course of action for everyone, which I doubt it is, the fact is that it's not a realistic suggestion. What is realistic is a concerted effort to try and counteract the effects of media manipulation so that you can try and gain a greater level of emotional stability and mental control.

Try and cut back on your media diet. Be pickier about the things you put into your mind. Practice a healthy skepticism when you encounter news stories that are designed to play upon your passions.

**Memento Mori**

Let us prepare our minds as if we'd come to the very end of life. Let us postpone nothing. Let us balance life's books each day... The one who puts the finishing touches on their life each day is never short of time.

—Seneca

The phrase "memento mori" is central to Stoic thought. It's Latin, translating roughly to "remember that you must die."

It's a stark phrase that brings us face to face with a fact of life that most of us would rather not deal with. You might be thinking that it's too morbid, and that it doesn't belong in a book about trying to free yourself from stress. After all, what could inspire more stress than the specter of death?

But you must remember that one of the fundamental practices of Stoicism is acceptance of fate. Like it or not, we all share a common fate. This is one of the reasons that a book written by someone as uniquely powerful as a Roman Emperor could inspire people from all walks of life.

Death is a constant for us all, no matter how rich or powerful we might be. It's a reminder that even though some people seem as though they have transcended beyond the realm of mere mortals through their talent, prestige, or beauty, in the end all must face death.

It isn't something any of us wants to accept, but practicing Stoicism means accepting difficult truths. But this doesn't mean that Stoicism is a morbid philosophy. Every honest philosophy must deal with death. The question is how they deal with death.

**Life After Death?**

At this point, some of you may be wondering what Stoicism has to say about the afterlife. After all, just about everyone agrees that death is inevitable, but almost no one can agree on what happens after death.

Here it's important to remember that Stoicism is a philosophy, not a religion. Throughout history Stoics have held many different religious beliefs. The earliest Stoics were Greek and Roman polytheists who believed in entire pantheons of gods. Then, when the Roman Empire converted to Christianity, many Christian thinkers combined Christian theology with Stoic ideas to create new ways of thinking about life. Today people of all faiths and beliefs can call themselves skeptics, each finding some way to combine Stoicism's ideas about this life with their religious convictions concerning the possibility of an afterlife.

Remember that stoicism is a practical philosophy. It's designed to answer the question of how we should act in this life. Nothing about Stoicism precludes the possibility of an afterlife, but it isn't married to the idea of one either.

This is one area where you have to reach your own conclusions. Just understand that whatever your beliefs might be, you are not alone in the Stoic community. It's a diverse and welcoming group that is open to people of every creed.

**Living in the Shadow of Death**

When people are first exposed to stoicism the idea of "memento mori" can often jump out as a belief that seems rather morbid and distasteful. This is understandable, it's easy to look at someone who is regularly thinks about the inevitability of death and assume that they are some sort of "death worshipper" who loves death more than life. But this can't be further from the case when it comes to the vast majority of Stoics.

The truth is that Stoics don't think of death because it's pleasant, we remind ourselves of death because it is unpleasant. It is the splash of cold water that wakes us up to the harsh reality, which is that life is limited.

Most Stoics love life. Without any certainty with regards to life after death we can only be confident that this life is our chance to live virtuously and seek constant improvement. The fact that death is inevitable is a reminder that we only have a finite amount of time available that we can achieve all the things that we want to achieve.

We don't remember death because we value death, we remember death because it reminds us how much we should value life. None of us knows how long our time on this earth will be. You might live to be 120 or you could die tomorrow. That's why it's important to make the most out of every moment, because you never know which moment will be your last.

**Practical Takeaway**

Death is something that no one wants to deal with, but we will all face one day. Stoics have always believed that accepting the realities of life is essential to living the best life possible. In this exercise, we will look at a healthy and productive way to deal with the topic of death.

Take out your paper and writing utensil. Now take a few moments to write down the eulogy that you would like to have read at your funeral someday.

Are you finished?

This is a classic exercise that is designed to help you focus in on what your real values are in this life. In a consumerist society it can be all too easy to get lost in a forest of material concerns. But when all is said and done, most people value relationships above even their most prized physical possessions.

Read over your eulogy and ask yourself how you feel about it. Do you feel like you have lived a life that you can be happy with when all is said and done? Or do you feel like the way you are living your life doesn't align with your deeper priorities?

Thinking about your own death isn't a pleasant activity, but it can help to focus your mind on what is truly important in your life.

# Chapter 7: Living in Accordance with Nature

*To a rational being it is the same thing to act according to nature and according to reason.*

—Marcus Aurelius

A Stoic is often understood to be someone who stands silently and endures pain and strife, but this is only part of a larger picture. Stoicism does teach us that we should endure difficulties when necessary, but the bigger point is that we should try and move with the flow of nature rather than fighting against it.

A life of Stoicism doesn't need to be a life of struggle. The Stoics have always sought to live a life of peace and harmony, where human choices are brought in line with nature.

## The Natural World, Inside and Out

The Stoic Sage is supposed to accept nature fully, both inside and out. This means that he accepts the human nature that governs him as an individual and society at large, while accepting the laws of nature that govern everything on this planet and across the universe. Life isn't a struggle for the Sage because they don't just begrudgingly accept nature, they move with its tides and are carried through life.

Before we get too far into this topic, it's important to take a moment to understand just what Stoics mean when they talk about nature. When modern individuals talk about nature, they picture the natural world, with plants, animals, and blue sky. But when Stoic philosophers considered nature, they were thinking about the fundamental characteristics of everything that exists.

So, when we talk about accepting nature that includes accepting the natural world around us, but it also means something that is simultaneously larger and more intimate.

**The Natural World**

One of the first and most important things that a Stoic must accept is the natural world that governs all life. We are only able to survive on this planet because the laws of nature allow for it. The Stoics also understood that while humans may be different from other lifeforms in some crucial ways, we still fit within the larger ecosystem like a piece that is placed into a large puzzle.

Reason demands that we respectfully accept the forces of nature and our own place within the large and impossibly complex natural world that we reside in. This may seem like another obvious suggestion, but you will find that people often have a hard time accepting the natural world.

Consider how many times you have heard people complaining about the basic laws of nature. This is something that's especially common when it comes to people who are trying to lose weight. Who hasn't wondered why unhealthy food seems to taste so great while unhealthy food seems so unappealing? After a hard day of working out just about anyone will feel compelled to ask why gaining weight is so easy while burning calories is so difficult.

We all feel the urge to complain about the many ways that the world can be frustrating. Stoicism teaches that we shouldn't feel bad about this natural urge, but it also says that we should not indulge it. When we feel the urge to complain about the laws of nature, we are to instead practice acceptance.

You must also remember that every time we feel frustrated, we have an opportunity to develop our personal virtue. Anyone can move smoothly through a life with no challenges, it requires a virtuous person to meet obstacles head on and overcome them without complaint.

This doesn't mean that you will always be able to deal with every frustrating fact of life with perfect grace but can strive to be like a Sage in everything you do. The goal is growth, as long as you constantly push yourself to grow and improve you are acting in accordance with Stoic virtue.

**Human Nature**

Another side of nature that every Stoic has to deal with is humanity. As humans, we share a common nature that connects us. We have our own individual natures, and then we have a collective nature that governs how we interact with one another in groups.

Long before anthropologists understood the importance of community to all human beings, the Stoics understood that, as humans, we are social creatures.

As Marcus Aurelius said, humans "were born for cooperation, like feet, like hands, like eyelids, like the rows of upper and lower teeth. So, to work in opposition to one another is against nature: and anger or rejection is opposition."

Not all of us are equally social in nature. Some people need more alone time while others require almost constant socialization. But human beings in general need strong social connections to live healthy and productive lives.

## Understanding and Acceptance

Many modern Stoics find that the practice of living in accordance with nature is one of the most difficult things to do.

There is no way around the full complexity of this matter, but there are shortcuts you can take to cut through some of the more technical questions and get down to the problems that are most relevant to our daily lives.

As a Stoic, your main task is to understand what you can change in this life so that you can accept the things that you currently cannot. One point that Stoic philosophy makes again and again is that we should not waste time and energy struggling to change things which cannot be changed. This is considered to be the height of folly and the downfall of many poor souls.

This is why Stoicism puts so much of an emphasis on personal action. So many things in this world are beyond our control, but if you look within yourself, you will find that you can achieve a great many things. You may not be able to rewrite the rules of modern society but if you are willing to do what is necessary you can dramatically change the way you live within this society.

## The Unnatural State of Modern Life

While the ancient Stoics weren't focused on things like blue skies and green fields when they discussed the power of nature, they were living in a world that was much different from the one we currently live in. Even in the bigger cities of Athens and Rome the Stoics never could have imagined a world as far from nature as the cities that modern human beings have created.

Stoicism isn't against humans making changes to their environment. Invention and innovation are essential parts of human nature, many Stoics would argue that to live a life without clothing, tools, or constructed housing would violate human nature. But there is also a point when humans move so far beyond the environments that we were shaped by that we are like fish that have been taken out of water. Many people who live solitary lives in dark rooms are practically drowning, denied so many of the things that their human nature yearns for on a fundamental level.

None of this is to suggest that Stoicism demands that you leave the city behind and head out to the countryside. The idea is humbler than that, what is needed is greater exposure to natural environments and a return to the more natural patterns of life that existed before humans began to try and transform the world.

Spend less time staring at images of the world on a computer screen and more time looking out at the world with your own two eyes. Take regular breaks from your compact apartments and offices to get out under the wide-open sky.

**The Importance of Sleep**

One especially crucial change to consider is your sleep schedule. Few modern people get as much sleep as they require. And even when people get enough sleep, they often experience low quality sleep that leaves them feeling tired and irritable as they go about their day.

The average person needs more sleep than they are getting. A study showed that "forty-five percent of Americans say that poor or insufficient sleep affected their daily activities" throughout the average week (National Sleep Foundation, 2014). There are also questions about sleep patterns. For most of human existence people went to bed sometime around sunset and woke up sometime around sunrise. This makes perfect sense when you consider the fact that most people had limited choices for lighting up the dark night, so there wasn't much they could do once the sun went down.

But thanks to the advent of electricity we can now extend our daily activities deep into the night. This might sometimes be good for our social lives, but it can cause trouble for our sleep schedules. Just because you can disobey your body's internal clock doesn't mean that you should. Getting in touch with the natural rhythms of your body is a good way to become happier, healthier, and more energetic.

**Food for Thought**

Another area you should seriously look into is your diet. The human body needs certain nutrients to do everything that it is designed to do. Trying to live without eating a diverse selection of nutritious food is like driving your car around without putting gas in your tank. Logic dictates that eventually you will be stranded along the side of the road.

You must accept that your body needs certain things if you want to live a healthy and productive life. Just as acceptance of reality is an essential prerequisite that must come before rational action, a good diet must come before healthy living. You can't have one without the other.

While Stoicism is focused on what human beings can achieve when they master control of their minds, it isn't a sort of mysticism that believes that the mind is somehow disconnected from the body. A healthy mind can help improve the condition of your body, but the same thing goes in reverse. If you don't take care of your body, then the condition of your mind will deteriorate.

### Cutting the Clutter and Finding Control

Modern advancements in the realms of science, technology, and medicine have improved our quality of life in so many ways. But in addition to the many positives we enjoy come plenty of draw backs.

For all the material luxuries we enjoy, many modern people feel suffocated. They go through life in a world that is tight, crowded, and far away from the clean and fresh air that our ancestors once enjoyed. We experience the world at a distance, gazing at simulations and recreations instead of experiencing things firsthand.

Life doesn't have to be this way. You don't have to be swept up by the crowds and carried into a future you want no part of. The power to make a change and chart your own course is within you. All you need to do is seize it.

### What Acceptance Doesn't Mean

While we are on the topic of acceptance, it is important to understand its limitations. Stoic acceptance simply means accepting the world as it is in the moment of the present. It doesn't mean that you have to love the world as it is or submit yourself to everything within it.

There might be pollution in the river near your house. Stoicism says that you should accept that the water is polluted. Does that mean that you should go down to the river and take a drink? No! Stoicism is about rational action; it will never call for you to do something so irrational and self-destructive.

For a deeper understanding of this concept, let's look at a great quote from Marcus Aurelius:

> *A cucumber is bitter. Throw it away. There are briars in the path. Turn aside from them. This is enough. Do not add: And why were such things put into the world?" For you will be ridiculed by a man who is acquainted with nature as you would be ridiculed by a carpenter and a shoemaker if you found fault because you found shavings and cuttings in their workshop from the things they make.*

What Aurelius is pointing out here is that too many people waste their energy railing against things that they cannot change. When you can take simple actions to avoid dealing with issues then you should take those actions and move on with your life. When you must endure frustrations then you should endure them silently and then move on with your life. Endlessly complaining about circumstances that are beyond your control only adds to your suffering, it doesn't make the world any more pleasant.

This quote also reminds us that Stoicism isn't always about enduring any unpleasant thing that is put in your path. If you don't want to eat a cucumber, then you don't need to eat it. If a certain pain is difficult to cross, you can find a different route. Being a Stoic means that you will endure unpleasant things when it is necessary, it doesn't mean that you have to seek out or submit yourself to every negative thing under the sun.

Stoicism is about finding peace through acceptance. It's about ceasing the endless struggle against the people and things that are beyond our control. The Stoic Sage transcends the struggles of everyday reality by accepting it as it is with such an open heart and mind that it loses the power to influence the Sage's thoughts in any way.

**Changing What You Can and Accepting What You Can't**

When Stoics talk about nature, they are considering the fundamental traits that make something what it is. This is mirrored in the way that we talk about the natural world that exists beyond human civilization. The birds, trees, and grass all existed before humans invented fire, and they will reclaim the Earth if humanity ever goes extinct.

Humanity's creations can be wonderful, but we shouldn't get so lost in ourselves that we think just because we can survive without something it means that we can live healthy lives without it. Across the world people are enjoying the latest creature comforts while slowly withering away due to a lack of basic natural resources.

You don't have to become a revolutionary to improve your quality of life. It's possible to accept many of the changes of modern life without abandoning the basic things that have always made healthy human lives possible.

Every Stoic must practice acceptance, but that doesn't mean that they shouldn't take action. Sometimes you need to accept that you have needs that aren't being fulfilled, and then act on those needs.

So, now is the time to ask yourself, are you living in harmony with your basic nature?

**Practical Takeaway**

In this modern world, all too many people are living out of sync with their natural needs.

Take out a piece of paper and writing utensil. Now write down all of the things that you think humans have needed to live healthy lives throughout human history.

Once you have a list down, look over the list and consider what areas your own life might be lacking. Circle them and then brainstorm ideas for how you might be able to address these concerns.

Stoicism puts a huge emphasis on thought, but Stoics

have always understood that humans are more than just our brains. Healthy thoughts are more likely to come from healthy bodies. So, start taking any steps you can to take care of yourself.

# Chapter 8: Stoicism and Psychology

*The things you think about determine the quality of your mind.*

—Marcus Aurelius

Since its creation, Stoicism has sought to explain how the human mind works and how it can be reshaped in our quest to live virtuous lives. When Stoicism first arose in ancient Greece it was the philosophers where were best equipped to dig into questions surrounding the human mind and the thoughts and feelings surrounding it.

But two thousand years have passed since the birth of philosophy and a lot has changed. While philosophers are still hard at work trying to understand the nature of human consciousness there has been a major shift that has rewritten the role of philosophy. Philosophy is no longer the primary way that we understand the human mind, now our fundamental understanding comes from the scientific study of our brains and thought patterns.

Fields of study such as psychology, biology, and neurology have reshaped the way that we think about thought. But this doesn't mean that philosophy is out of the game! Read on to find out how modern Stoics deal with the latest revelations produced by the scientists who have unlocked the secrets of the human mind.

## Ancient Philosophy Meets Modern Science

The human brain is an incredibly complex thing. Since the advent of the scientific method we have come to understand many things about how the brain works, but every question we have answered has raised many others.

Still, we can say certain things about the human brain that the ancient Stoics weren't able to. The ancient Greeks were incredibly intelligent and understood more than many modern individuals give them credit for. Still, they had no way of knowing how the mind worked. As such, many philosophers had beliefs about human thought that might clash with modern science.

One area of contention is the question of "free will." Philosophers have long argued that humans can achieve full control over their mind simply by force of thought. The idea was that there was an immaterial mind or spirit that reigned over the physical body, operating it outside of the normal chain of cause and effect that governs most of the physical realm.

This belief makes intuitive sense. Most people feel as

though they are in complete control. But centuries of scientific studies have shown us a different side of human thought.

## The Importance of Brain Chemistry

One of the most confounding questions that humans have had to ask themselves is how the thoughts we think and the emotions we feel are connected to our physical bodies. There once was a time when people believed that thoughts were completely immaterially, totally detached from our physical forms. But as we have been able to look closer into the human brain we have witnessed surprising connections.

For one thing, it seems as if alterations made to the brain can affect the way people think and feel. One of the most compelling displays of the impact that brain physiology has on human choice and personality is the case of Phineas Gage.

Gage was a railroad construction worker back in the 1800s. By all accounts he was a polite and pleasant individual until the day when an explosion sent an iron rod flying through the air and into Gage's head. By all accounts the accident should have been deadly, but Gage was miraculously able to survive with the large piece of metal stuck in his brain (O'Driscoll).

But while Gage's body lived through the accident many close to him felt that the Gage they knew died in the accident. Phineas underwent a rapid change in his personality. The once friendly man became vulgar and rude. Damage to his brain seemed to turn him into a completely different person, and suddenly people began to think differently about the link between physiology and identity.

While further study has shown that some of the grander claims made about Gage's transformation were exaggerated, his story is just one example of many where changes in brain composition have led to marked changes in thinking, decision making, and personality.

Such recent scientific revelations have caused modern Stoics to rethink some of the ancient beliefs surrounding human thought. The ancient Stoics believed that any person could achieve total control over their brain if they followed Stoic prescriptions to the letter. Today people are more skeptical of this proposition, understanding that every individual has a unique brain composition that might predispose them in certain directions.

This means that some people may find that the Stoic approach comes easily to them, while others will have an especially difficult time trying to wrestle with their natural dispositions. This calls for a careful reexamination of Stoic thought, but it doesn't strike at the core of stoicism. Maybe not everyone can become a Sage, but that doesn't mean that people can't seek to progress from where they are.

## A Change in Thinking

One way that modern neuroscience supports the Stoic system is the complexity it has revealed within the human mind. The old beliefs that suggested human minds were relatively simple and easy to control have been replaced with a more nuanced understanding of everything that adds up to create human consciousness.

Some people believe that modern revelations about the complex web of factors that influences our decision making is dehumanizing. This is understandable, when you're brought up to believe that you are in complete control of every thought and action it can be disturbing to realize that there are so many things that shape our choices without our conscious knowledge. But is this dehumanizing?

I would propose that this information is imply revealing a new layer of what it means to be human. The fact that we didn't recognize our full complexity in the past does not mean that we were ever simple creatures who had total control. We have always had complex and contradictory minds, and science now allows us to understand the reasons behind the struggles that have been going on since the days of ancient Stoics and back into the dawn of humanity.

Finally, Stoicism reminds us all of the dangers of reacting negatively to reality. You may not like the world, but your preferences will not rewrite reality. Pretending as if brain chemistry doesn't exist won't give you greater control over your thoughts and actions. On the contrary, if you're unwilling to face the all-too-real factors that shape your thinking then you are actually tying your hands behind your back, limiting our options in an age where we as humans are being given the chance to take charge of our future.

## Cognitive Behavioral Therapy

One area where ancient stoicism and modern science are in remarkable alignment is the practice of Cognitive Behavioral Therapy, or CBT.

CBT is an approach to therapy that seeks to help people by changing their thinking patterns. The idea is that the thoughts we think, the emotions we feel, and the way we feel are all interconnected, and that changes made to one link in this chain can dramatically change the entire system.

Many people end up in a vicious downward spiral because they create negative feedback loops. They think negative thoughts, which leads them to feel negative emotions, which leads to destructive actions. As the person deals with the fallout from their poor choices their negative self-view is reinforced and the cycle begins again, only this time everything is even more vicious than it was before.

This sort of behavior is all too common, and anyone who has experienced such a downward spiral can understand how hopeless the situation might seem. But CBT and Stoicism both offer a way out of this cycle.

You see, both CBT and Stoicism propose that a holistic change can be brought about if individuals can take control of their thoughts. Suddenly the spiral becomes reversed, as positive thoughts lift up emotion and action and counteract the old negativity.

This is just the start of the similarities. Stoicism and CBT share a similar outlook, a shared emphasis on action, and the prioritization of clear and rational thinking. By studying the parallels between philosophy and therapy you can see how ancient ideas are leading to solid results in the world of modern science.

## The Importance of Action

Stoicism is an action-centered philosophy and CBT is an action-centered approach to therapy. Both believe that in order to bring about real change needs to come from inside the person who wants to grow. In addition, the change won't come from learning alone. Wisdom is important, but no one internalizes the information they learn until they put it into practice.

While both Stoicism and CBT start with changes to the way people think, the ultimate proof of change is seen in the way they act. People are always quick to say they have learned their lesson, but then when they are asked to put their new knowledge into practice they fall apart. The Stoics understood that learning is a process that takes time. Whether you're in therapy for a psychological disorder or simply looking to gain more control of your life, until changes start to manifest in your actions you won't see the full impact of what you've learned.

## The Importance of Clear Thinking

Another link between CBT and Stoicism is the emphasis on clear and careful thinking. All sorts of problems can arise when you don't see the world as it is. Even people who are blessed with a mind that is free from disorders or similar issues can still develop a distorted view of the world for many reasons. The situation is more pronounced when issues arise within the physical makeup of the brain. But no matter how deep the issue is, CBT has shown that steps can be taken to correct patterns of thought.

Of course, some people will have greater difficulties achieving clear thought than others. This is one area where modern science corrects some of the ancient thinkers. Once upon a time people blamed people with mental disorders for their issues. They thought that if such individuals just worked harder, they'd be like everyone else. Science has shown us that this isn't the case.

The delicate brain chemistry within each of us can go wrong easily. This is why just about everyone will confess that they are struggling with their own issues if you get them to open up. Some of these issues are more severe than others, but we could all use help breaking free from our mental traps and seeing more clearly. Stoicism outlined this all those years ago, and today CBT offers people a concrete path to clearer thought.

**Combining Therapy and Philosophy**

Human beings are complex creatures. We are rarely satisfied with one-dimensional solutions. We hunger for both reason and emotion. This is why the combination of CBT and Stoicism can be a powerful combination.

Many people can appreciate the science of CBT and the intellectual pedigree that just about any practitioner brings to the table. But people can still be left yearning for more. Most people long to be part of something bigger than themselves, something that can help connect them with a grand tradition. This is one of the reasons that religious belief and patriotism are such powerful forces, they bring people together as part of a tradition that stretches back into the past.

Stoicism is a secular belief system that can offer people the history and beauty that they are longing for. It's a two-thousand-year-old philosophy that is supported by some of the most beautiful and moving writing ever produced by Western Philosophy. It combines intellectualism and romanticism into a package that is still drawing people thousands of years after its founder passed away.

When the emotional power of Stoicism combines with the scientific appeal of CBT, wonderful things can happen. But beyond the practical level, it also serves as a reminder of just how amazing those original Stoics were. Even with all of the advances in knowledge that have occurred since the days of ancient Greece we are still using their wisdom to light our way forward.

### Working with Your Unique Brain Chemistry

The ancient Stoics had some understanding of the variety that existed among human beings, but they couldn't have known the deep-seated nature of these differences. The idea that we might have biochemical software like DNA guiding our actions or complex electro-chemical reactions in our brain shaping our thoughts was far beyond their ability to discover.

This doesn't mean that modern learners need to throw out the work of the ancients. A careful study of the foundational Stoic works reveals that while the writers may not have known what we now do about the physical makeup of the human mind they still produced ideas and theories that align remarkably well with the latest in scientific advances.

In 2015 a counselor by the name of Ian Guthrie led his patients through a discussion of Marcus Aurelius' Meditations. He found that while his patients were "seriously and persistently mentally ill" his patients benefited from a guided discussion of the topic. (Guthrie 2015)

This goes to show that all kinds of people can benefit from studying and practicing Stoicism. You may feel that you might be held back by the circumstances of your birth or negative situations you've experienced throughout your life, but none of this means that you can't gain a greater understanding of yourself and a stronger control over your mind through a study of Stoicism. Some people are certainly more privileged than others, but all can gain if they commit themselves to following the wisdom passed down from the ancient Stoics.

## A Word of Caution

At this point it's worth reiterating the point that this

is not a medical book. While some people report that practicing Stoic behavior and thoughts has improved their quality of life that does not mean that this philosophy or any other is a replacement for medical treatment. If you have physical or mental health issues, then your first priority should be seeing a trained medical professional who can help you get your situation under control.

While modern Stoics disagree about many things, one area where there is wide agreement is that true Stoicism must be in line with the latest in scientific discoveries. The ancient Stoics were able to develop many incredible insights into the nature of the human mind long before the creation of the modern scientific method, but that is no reason to take their word over the latest discoveries from scientists and medical professionals.

**Science and Stoicism: Working Together**

Stoicism is about improving your mind, and we can all be thankful that science has given us incredible insights into how the mind works, how it can go wrong, and how we can improve it through a wide array of approaches. Therapy, medication, exercise, and many other options can all be used to improve your mental health and allow you to take control of your life.

You should never feel like you have to choose between Stoicism and the treatments proposed by trained medical professionals. Modern Stoics are overwhelmingly pro-science and are constantly working to integrate the latest discoveries into their understanding of stoicism. When science and philosophy work together incredible things can happen, don't ever feel like you have to choose between one or the other in your search for a happier and healthier life.

**Practical Takeaway**

Thought is one of those things that comes so naturally that we just take it for granted. But if you want to take control of your thoughts then it helps to take some time to examine how you think.

For this exercise you will need to find a quiet, peaceful place.

Once you have an area to yourself and a few minutes to spare you can use meditation to examine the inner workings of your mind.

Close your eyes, breathe slowly, and count down slowly from ten with each exhale. Once you get to one just keep repeating that number. This will help to quiet your conscious inner monologue.

Take the time to be in the moment and observe how your mind reacts. Watch how thoughts enter into your mind. Feel as your body reacts to the peace and quiet.

So many of us spend our days with thoughts running constantly though our mind, but we never really examine just how these thoughts come to us. This sort of meditation isn't just a good way to calm down and take a break from the chaos of modern life, it will also give you a deeper understanding of how your mind works.

# Chapter 9: Accepting the Unacceptable

*It does not matter what you bear, but how you bear it.*

—Seneca

Throughout this book we have looked at the most fundamental principles of Stoicism and how you can use these principles to navigate the ups and downs of your daily life. But what happens when you face struggles that go beyond the ordinary?

No one on this earth can live a life free from tragedy. That is why any philosophy must wrestle with the true depths of human suffering. Anyone can come up with a way to make sense of an easy life, it takes true wisdom to find a path forward when suffering becomes so deep that we feel driven to despair.

## Dealing with Pain and Suffering

Throughout this book we have come time and time again to the different ways that Stoics handled pain, disappointment, and other forms of suffering. But so far, we've mainly looked at the sort of problems that cause us trouble but don't shake us to the bone.

What happens when a Stoic feels the sort of pain that might destroy a person?

It's one thing to look for opportunities in the little setbacks that we suffer every day, but what about real instances of tragedy? Sometimes it can feel as if our philosophies fall apart when we face down suffering on a major scale. When pain tears us apart and it feels like no one else has ever suffered so much all the wisdom in the world can ring hollow.

**You're Not Alone**

The first thing to understand is that no matter what you are going through, you aren't the first person to suffer as you are. Your situation may be unique, but pain and suffering are as old as humanity.

This is why we look to the wisdom of the ancients in these matters. Everything feels new when we are experiencing it ourselves, but the truth is that the same emotions have played out over and over again for countless generations. One of the things that joins humanity together is our shared suffering.

The next thing to understand is that while some forms of pain might feel so extraordinary that normal advice doesn't hold true, the fact is that these are the situations where it's absolutely crucial that we cling to whatever wisdom we have. When the first wave of pain hits you it might feel like you can never recover, but just because you feel this way doesn't make it true. You can still practice Stoicism and refuse to dwell on what you've experienced. It may take every ounce of strength that you can draw from every fiber of your being, but if you can do it then you can stop the bleeding and prevent the situation from becoming worse than it has to.

This sort of pain and suffering is the reason why it is so valuable to practice Stoicism in everything that you do. You do not want to have to learn the art of acceptance while you are dealing with something that seems patently unacceptable. You need to start small and create a habit of acceptance that can grow over time until one day it might carry you through times of pain and strife.

**It's Never Too Early to Prepare for Pain**

If you are going through a relatively positive period in your life you may feel like you can skim through all of this. When life is going well the human mind has a way of assuming that things will continue to go well forever. But the fact is that every life has ups and downs. Everyone experiences good and bad times. If you are experiencing a good period right now, then one of the best things you can do is prepare for when your fortune shifts

"It is in times of security that the spirit should be preparing itself for difficult times; while fortune is bestowing favors on it is then is the time for it to be strengthened against her rebuffs."-Seneca

No one enjoys misfortune. But those who are used to misfortune are much better prepared to handle it than those who have never experienced it. This is why people born into poverty aren't as likely to be destroyed by it as those who were born into wealth and then dropped low by fate.

The good news is that you don't actually have to inflict harm upon yourself to prepare yourself for the pain that might come in the future. You can begin to prepare yourself through the Stoic practice of visualization. Picture things going wrong. But don't just stop there. Imagine what you might do if your fortunes were to change. Think of how you could turn misfortune into opportunity.

You see, if you just visualize pain then you are only likely to depress yourself. But if you push past the pain you can remember the essential truth of Stoicism, that every moment is an opportunity to develop your virtue.

This may not redeem suffering in your eyes or explain why you have to go through it. But Stoicism isn't about explaining why things happen. Stoics don't ask why fate deals us the cards it deals; Stoics just take what they are given and make the best of the situation.

## *Processing Grief*

Of all the kinds of pain that humanity is forced to bear, none is more fearsome than grief. Grief is the dragon that lays low even the mightiest hearts.

It is hard to put into words the enormity of grief, but that doesn't mean that it is beyond you. Grief is something that almost nobody can fathom, and yet everyone must learn to deal with it at some point in their life.

Even if you can't imagine how Stoicism can help you deal with grief you must trust that it can. You have the power inside of you, and if you can practice the wisdom of the Sage you can overcome any obstacle.

For instruction on how to handle grief, we can look to Seneca.

"Nature requires from us some sorrow, while more than this is the result of vanity. But never will I demand of you that you should not grieve at all. ... Let your tears flow, but let them also cease, let deepest sighs be drawn from your breast, but let them also find an end."

The first thing to remember is that a stoic isn't someone who doesn't feel pain. If you feel pain in the wake of a great loss it doesn't mean that you aren't a Stoic, it simply means that you are human.

What separates Stoics from others is how they process pain.

No matter how bad the pain feels you need to practice the Stoic art of clear and rational thinking. You must be able to step back and realize that even if it feels like the pain will last forever, the reality is that everything in this life is impermanent. This too will pass.

It may feel like the pain will never go away, but the truth is that it will dull with time. It may never fully disappear, but it won't always threaten to swallow you whole. This is the sort of thing you must remember and take solace in.

Finally, remember that Stoicism teaches that we can wrestle control of our emotions and redirect them. You can take negative emotions and move them in a healthier direction. You can spend your days dwelling on the pain you feel after losing someone, or you can think about how lucky you are that you were able to experience life with them while they were with you.

There is never just one thing that we must feel. We always have a choice that we can make. Wallowing in pain is something that you have to choose. You can also choose to pull yourself up out of your sorrow and move towards something more constructive. It isn't easy and it doesn't happen quickly, but the sooner you start moving the sooner you will reach your destination.

## Wrestling with Big Questions

Once again, at this stage it is worth acknowledging the limitations of Stoicism. While Stoicism has the answers to many of life's pressing questions, there are other areas where things are left open to interpretation.

What is the ultimate meaning of life? Is there a God? Does anything happen to us after we die?

These are all deep, meaningful, and highly personal questions that modern Stoicism shies away from.

Some of you may feel like this is a cop-out, but the

truth is that it comes from a place of intellectual humility. There are modern Stoics who belong to every system of belief imaginable, religious or otherwise. Each finds a way to marry Stoic thought with their personal convictions so that they can make sense of the world around them and get through the ups and downs of each day.

In the end, Stoicism isn't about answering every question. It's about how you make your way through life. Questions that go beyond this are also beyond the scope of this book.

**Letting Go**

The one thing that Stoicism tells us clearly in this area is that acceptance is key. This is one of those areas where acceptance is incredibly difficult, but that's why it's so important. No one wants to accept or acknowledge loss, but it's a step that must be taken before the healing process can begin.

Nothing in Stoicism may take the sting out of grief, but if you practice Stoic acceptance you may find that you are better prepared to accept even the most agonizing truths when the time comes. Acceptance is like any other skill, practice makes perfect. The sooner you start coming to grips with reality in all its ugliness and glory, the better prepared you will be for the worst blows that life might throw your way.

The pain of loss will stay around for as long as you hold onto it. Stoicism teaches us that all pain can be removed if we bring ourselves to let go. It's never easy, but it is the right thing to do. Until you let go, you can't move forward.

## Interacting with Others

If you fully commit to practicing Stoicism you will witness as certain transformations take place in your life. With time your way of seeing the world will change, as will the manner in which you think and feel. As time passes and you internalize more and more Stoic thought you may find that others look at you different, with some acquaintances wondering if you are the same person they once knew.

One thing that committed Stoics realize is that it can feel like there is a gap between them and the average person, a gap that widens with time. The fact of the matter is that most people are not Stoics. Even though Stoic wisdom could benefit everyone, most people will never embrace this philosophy.

With this in mind, it's worth considering how Stoics should act around non-Stoics. If you want to live a productive and pleasant life you need to think carefully and act thoughtfully.

### Living in a World Full of Non-Stoics

Stoicism is all about acceptance, and one thing that every Stoic needs to accept is that not everyone shares their beliefs. Maybe the world would be a better place if everyone was a Stoic, but chances are that such a world will never come to be.

This means that as a Stoic you must understand that

not everyone will think like you or share your values.

For example, your personal slogan might be "memento mori" and you might find that constant reminders of your own mortality are a good way to encourage productivity and a meaningful life. This doesn't mean that those around you will appreciate being reminded that they are going to die someday.

Whenever someone is introduced to a new belief system that speaks to them in a deep and profound way their first impulse is usually to share their newfound wisdom with everyone they can. This is a natural and understandable impulse, but it can also be hazardous.

**Stoic Empathy**

One way that Stoicism can help you deal with those around you is the empathy that it can help you develop. Once you seriously commit to working to address your own shortcomings and weaknesses you can gain an appreciation for the struggles that other people are going through. Digging deep within yourself will reveal the root causes of bad behavior, and once you understand this in yourself, you'll be able to see it in others.

Suddenly you'll be able to watch as someone insults you or cuts you off without being insulted the way you once were. This is because you understand that this sort of behavior isn't usually about you, it's a reflection of the inner struggles the other person is dealing with.

Finally, the more you practice Stoicism the better equipped you will be to maintain your calm in the face of negative circumstances.

## Practicing Stoic Humility

I want you to consider once more the idea that we should accept fate. Stoicism calls on us to accept fate because so much in this life is beyond our control. We then move from acceptance of fate to focus in on taking command of our thoughts, emotions, and actions.

But what if we think more about fate? Consider just how much is beyond your control. The universe is a giant place and you only have control over your body and some of the things that it comes in contact with.

Properly understood, Stoicism is incredibly humbling. Even a great emperor like Marcus Aurelius came to understand his limitations through Stoicism. Other Emperors saw themselves as deities, but Marcus understood that he was really no different than any other man.

The Stoic understands that our control is extremely limited, but we are still incredibly fortunate to be blessed with what we have. Life may be filled with struggles, but it is also all too brief. That is why we must make the most of every moment we have on this planet.

## Practical Takeaway

All life is temporary. This is a painful fact of life. Still, it is one of the things that makes life so precious. The fact that those closest to us will not be with us forever should remind us to cherish our time with them while they are here.

Take out a piece of paper and writing utensil. Think of someone you care about. Realize that they will not be with you forever.

Now write a message to them. Let them know just how much they mean to you.

You can give the letter to them, tell them the message with your own mouth, or keep the message private. The choice is yours alone.

Some Stoic practices may look morbid at first glance, but if you understand them in their proper context you will see that they are life-affirming. So many words go unsaid because people operate under the assumption that there will always be another day, another chance to meet. The truth is that life flies by, so you need to take advantage of every opportunity you're given.

Don't live in regret, let people know how you feel about them before it's too late.

# Chapter 10: Stoicism in Practice

*While we wait for life, life passes.*

—Seneca

Understanding the philosophical underpinnings can help you reorient your way of thinking, but if you want to see real change in your life then you need to take practical action. The word action here doesn't have the same meaning it does in phrases like "action movie," instead it refers to

Remember, stoicism isn't just a way of thinking about life. Stoicism is a way of living life. If you spend all day reading the great works of stoic literature but never put anything you've read into practice, then you'll be no better off than someone who has never heard the word before.

In this chapter we will look at some of the more practical steps that you can take to develop your stoic skills. You'll learn to take time to think things through, live with discomfort, and practice forward momentum. These steps can ensure that you achieve real results in your stoic journey.

# Separating Input and Action

Every computer program runs off of a long chain of inputs and actions. One calculation leads to another until a result is achieved. Every time you run a computer program or open up an app on your phone countless mathematical equations are run to produce everything you see play out on the screen in front of you.

The human mind is often compared to a computer, but the amazing thing is that we possess the ability to reprogram our own software. By thinking carefully about the way our mind works, observing our mind at work, and actively training ourselves, we can use our minds to transform our minds.

But what really separates man from machine is the value of quick thinking. While quick reactions are essential in computing, if humans think too quickly, they can get themselves in a lot of trouble.

Wisdom comes when you are able to think things through before you act.

"Between stimulus and response, there is a space. In that space is our power to choose our response."

-Viktor Frankl

In our natural state the gap between input and action is almost nonexistent. Anyone who has raised a child knows how often they will act without any forethought. It's only through education, personal experience, and the passage of time that people develop the ability to truly think through our choices.

But not everyone's thinking develops equally. Most people learn enough restraint to avoid ingesting poisonous cleaning products just because they look like candy. But how many people thoughtlessly fill their bodies with food that they know is poisoning them in more subtle ways?

The fact is that everyone could spread out the time between input and action in their lives. It's valuable to think of your mind as a muscle. If you want to be able to hold a heavy weight for a long time, then you need to practice lifting heavier and heavier weights until your muscles become strong enough for the task at hand. The same goes for your mental muscles. By practicing patience, restraint, and forethought at every opportunity you get you can develop this capacity.

It's important to remember that as it is with developing physical strength, it can take a long time to develop mental strength. You might have to work for years just to buy yourself a few seconds between action and reaction. Still, any world-class athlete will tell you that sometimes one second is the difference between losing the race and breaking a world record. Never underestimate the power of the slight edges you can gain over your competition.

You must also remember that just reading this book won't do anything to make you a more patient and thoughtful person, just as reading a book on weightlifting won't make you a physically stronger person. If you want to see real results, then you need to put the principles in this book into action.

If you can bring yourself to actually practice patience and put more thought into each action, then you can achieve incredible things. The world is filled with people who act without thinking, every bit of restraint that you can muster will help set you apart from the crowd. See for yourself.

### Embracing Discomfort/Practicing Misfortune

Human beings fear many things, but one of the most powerful drives behind all human behavior is the fear of loss. We are deathly afraid of losing what we have. Sometimes this drive produces positive results, but more often than not all it does is create stress and pain without preparing us for actual loss.

The Stoics understood this. They saw how many people lived lives of fear because they had become accustomed to a certain quality of life and couldn't imagine living if they were to lose their wealth and privilege.

Seneca was one of these philosophers. He saw the fear that gripped those around him and recognized it in himself. As a Stoic he knew that he needed to find a way to deal with this problem. The solution he devised was shocking, but undeniably powerful.

"Set aside a certain number of days during which you shall be content with the scantiest and cheapest fare, with coarse and rough dress, saying to yourself the while, 'Is this the condition that I feared?'"

Radical words. Words that are easier said than done. But according to the historical record Seneca practiced what he preached. From time to time he would leave behind the safety and security of his normal life behind and go out onto the streets to live like the poor and suffering Roman underclass.

Some may be offended by this idea, calling it "poverty tourism." They might, quite rightly, point out that there's a big difference between sleeping on the street for one night knowing that you have a home to return to in the morning and living with the ongoing pain and uncertainty of chronic homelessness. But these arguments miss the point.

Seneca wasn't trying to suggest that poor people have nothing to complain about or show off the fact that he can do anything he could do. As a Stoic he wasn't interested in proving himself to others, he was focused on cultivating his own mind. He discovered his own fears regarding deprivation and decided to face them head on.

Following stoicism doesn't mean that you must give up all your worldly comforts and live a life of poverty and deprivation. Stoicism is about recognizing that if, for some reason, you were plunged into a life of poverty and deprivation you could survive. Beyond that, it's about cultivating your personal virtues so that you might even thrive in such extreme circumstances.

## How to Practice Discomfort

Take a minute to think about the things in this world that you can't live without. Now narrow that list down to thinks that you might morally be allowed to give up. You shouldn't abandon your family just to try and build your own character.

If you're like most people, you'll have a list of things that are nice to have but ultimately unessential. Smart phones, televisions, expensive drinks, fancy clothes, and so on. Dig down as deep as you can, you may be surprised to discover just how many luxuries you enjoy as someone who lives in the modern world.

Now look at that list and imagine life without each item. Pay attention to how your body reacts. Is there anything that has such a hold on you that your heart starts beating faster just thinking about a day without it? The more afraid you are of living without something, the more valuable it would be to try and live without it.

I can already tell that plenty of you reading this area already making excuses. You'll say that you need this gadget for your work, or if you don't dress the right way you might miss out on some opportunity, and on and on. And your objections might be logical! But you need to know that the human mind is deathly afraid of loss and will do anything it can to hold onto what it has. That's why you need to ask yourself whether you are really acting in your own best interest or allowing fear to control you?

With most things on your list it might be helpful to

remember that there was a time when you didn't have your current luxuries. If you're on the younger side you might have to think back to when you were a child to recall the days before you always had a smartphone on you, but even if you have to go all the way back to infancy it still proves that once upon a time you could life without a constant internet connection. It's also worth recalling that many of history's greatest miracles were achieved by people who lacked our modern luxuries, or even our modern necessities!

Does this mean you have to give up everything and wander off into the woods? Not at all. As we've talked about when discussing willpower, human development takes time. And while some people can afford to give up everything and coast through life most of us don't have the privilege or constitution for such radical change.

What we all can do is make small but meaningful changes that remind us of what we really need in this life.

Maybe your job means that you need to be on-call at all times. Alright, but does that mean you need all the modern games and gadgets built into your latest smartphone? Could you stay in touch with work using a flip phone or even a pager?

We can also look to Seneca as an example of how we might practice discomfort. He lived life normally for the majority of the year, only sacrificing one day a month as a reminder of what was possible. Maybe you don't feel comfortable living life on the absolute bottom rung of society for even a day, but you could still dedicate one day a month to living with as little as possible.

When most people think about giving up luxuries, they focus on how their life will be constrained. Images of what they won't be able to do flash before their eyes. When your days are filled with modern entertainment it's easy to think that you'll have nothing at all to do if you give it up.

But a funny thing usually happens when people give up modern luxuries, they realize that they aren't all they're cracked up to be.

Sure, the smartphone has opened up a world of amazing opportunities. But it has also brought about plenty of unforeseen negative consequences. Remember that stoic thought isn't about labeling things like smart phones as good or evil, it's about seeing them as they are. And what they are is complicated and ultimately unnecessary.

If every smart phone in the world disappeared tomorrow, life would go on. The same goes for every other luxury item you can imagine. Remember that even the Great Emperors of Rome lived without electricity, gasoline, the internet, or modern medicine. If people back then could live without things that we sensibly label as essential, then how difficult would life really be if we learned to go without things that we all consider to be luxuries?

## Facing Your Fear

Some may view this whole concept as a form of masochism or insanity. After all, who in their right mind knowingly subjects themselves to pain and discomfort?

And yet we all go to the doctor to get our flu shots even though there's nothing pleasant about getting a needle shoved into our skin.

No one gets a shot because they like getting a shot, they get them because they know it will prepare them for what is to come. The same goes for the stoic. They don't seek out discomfort because they love discomfort, they seek it out because they know it's a fact of life. Discomfort will come, the question is whether or not you will be prepared.

## *Constant Forward Motion*

The stoic aims for constant development. Though they accept things as they are, they know that they can always work toward something greater.

This is something that just about any modern fan of stoicism will tell you. However, it can also be misleading. You must remember that the aims of a stoic are not the aims of the average person.

Most people think that in order to improve their life they must continually accumulate greater material wealth. Many people think that unless they're constantly adding up numbers they're falling behind in life. The stoic rejects all of this.

Stoicism is about understanding that life will have ups and downs. Actually, it's greater than that. Every true stoic remembers that life will end in death. With this in mind, they recognize the ultimate futility of the never-ending treadmill that so much of society seems to run on.

So, when the stoic talks about constant development and improvement, they are talking about working on themselves. They are constantly striving to train their thoughts, sharpen their mind, and strengthen their soul. This is because the stoic understands that the only thing, we truly possess in this world is ourselves.

**The Importance of Routine**

Let us return to one of the principle concepts of stoicism, the idea of living in tune with nature. Remember that this isn't about becoming a naturalist or luddite, it's about working with nature rather than against it. And the most important natural force we must all live with is human nature.

Every human being must learn to live with their natural inclinations. Just about no one lives a live free from the temptation to do things that are wrong. It's so tempting to make poor decisions, and poor decisions can quickly turn into bad habits.

This is why it's worth investing the time and energy needed to develop positive routines. It's a law of the universe that order tends to degrade into disorder with time. Only by inserting energy into the system can you preserve order, let alone build something larger and grander. If you aren't willing to invest in constant improvement, then you will have to settle for a slow descent into oblivion.

This is why you should set up a life filled with routines that will continually propel you towards a better life. The idea is that you can use the power of habit to make sure that you stay on the right track even when your willpower fails you.

Studies have shown that it takes around two months on average to create a new habit (Clear, 2018). That's why you should start integrating Stoic-inspired activities into your routine as soon as possible. The sooner you start practicing the sooner they will come to you naturally.

Practical Takeaway

You don't have to give up everything you own to get some taste of what it would be like to live without them. All you need is some creativity.

Take out your paper and writing utensil. Write down all the things you feel like you couldn't live without. Read the list over until you have it in your memory.

Now close your eyes and imagine life without anything on the list. Think through the consequences and how you would handle them. Try and project yourself as far into the future as possible.

So, how was it? Did you imagine yourself collapsing and giving up on life? Did you imagine yourself dying? Or was it possible that life might go on even without all that you rely upon and cherish?

The fact is that you are made out of stronger stuff than you might think. You do not need all of the things you feel like you need. If you are willing to try and do without these things, then you will see this firsthand. However, you can also learn this lesson through visualization. The choice is yours.

# Conclusion: A Philosophy for Life

There you have it. You now possess all of the basic tools necessary to start transforming your life. Still, you must keep in mind what this transformation entails.

The life of a Stoic is not an easy life. It isn't a perfect life, free from pain and setbacks. It isn't the life for those who dream of overnight success.

What Stoicism offers is a life of constant, gradual improvement. It's a slow and steady climb towards the peak of the mountain that exists within the human heart.

What you will come to discover as you practice Stoicism is that much of the pain and suffering experienced in life isn't mandatory but is actually self-inflicted. You cannot control the bad cards that fate might deal you, but with careful practice you can take command of the way your mind reacts to these situations.

Once you learn to stop dwelling on the downsides of situations and start looking for opportunities to grow as a person you can greatly increase your quality of life, decrease your level of stress, and achieve a calm that you might have never thought was possible.

Of course, these great changes will not happen

overnight. There is a large gap between accepting the proposition that suffering can be transcended and actually putting that idea into action. Stoicism isn't a miracle tonic that will transform you overnight, it is a lifestyle that must be practiced and perfected over the course of your life.

This might seem like a daunting proposition, but you must remember that this is the course of all true human self-improvement. There are no silver bullets that will instantly shoot down the obstacles in your path. The only people who consistently get rich off of "get rich quick" schemes are those that sell them to people who don't have any patience. The tried and true paths to success all involve hard work, commitment, and perseverance.

However, this doesn't mean that you will have to wait for months or years to start seeing results. If you have carefully read through the book and taken the knowledge within it to heart, then you should already see the world with new eyes. When you shift your perspective from one of pessimism and frustration to one of faith in endless opportunity then you can see wondrous changes occur in your life.

The world is filled with people who feel as though life has defeated them. They look around and decide that they have no hope because the world is against them. Many of these people are dealing with real prejudice that they must struggle to overcome, but many others are actually fighting against their own unhealthy attitude. And in both cases, negativity is holding them back from achieving their full potential.

A calmer, cooler, and more controlled you is possible. After reading this book you have all the tools you need to take command of your life. The only question is whether or not you'll do what it takes to achieve your goals.

# References

Clear, James. (2018). How Long Does It Take to Form a Habit? Backed by Science. Retrieved from jamesclear.com/new-habit.

Guthrie, Ian. (2015). Is Stoicism for the Mentally Ill, Too? Retrieved from modernstoicism.com/3934-2/.

Lack of Sleep Is Affecting Americans, Finds the National Sleep Foundation. (2014). Retrieved from www.sleepfoundation.org/press-release/lack-sleep-affecting-americans-finds-national-sleep-foundation.

Largay, James. (2014). James Largay: In His Life, U.S. Grant Was a Failure, a Butcher and a Savior. Retrieved from www.mcall.com/opinion/mc-ulysses-grant-death-anniversary-largay-yv-0724-20160723-story.html.

"Marcus Aurelius Antoninus." (n.d.). Encyclopedia of World Biography. Retrieved from https://www.encyclopedia.com/people/history/ancient-history-rome-biographies/marcus-aurelius.

O'Driscoll, K, and J.P. Leach. (1998) ""No longer Gage": an iron bar through the head. Early observations of personality change after injury to the prefrontal cortex. 1673-4. doi:10.1136/bmj.317.7174.1673a

Pigliucci, Massimo. (n.d.). Internet Encyclopedia of

Philosophy. Retrieved from www.iep.utm.edu/stoicism/.

Pigliucci, Massimo. (2017). "On the Nature of the Stoic Sage." Retrieved from brewminate.com/on-the-nature-of-the-stoic-sage/.

"Who Was Marcus Aurelius? An Introduction to the Last Great Emperor, Leader and Stoic of Rome." (n.d.). Retrieved from fs.blog/marcus-aurelius/.

www.ingramcontent.com/pod-product-compliance
Lightning Source LLC
Chambersburg PA
CBHW071737080526
44588CB00013B/2061